The Super Saleswoman

Janet Macdonald is an accountant by profession and a business woman by inclination. She received her education at grammar school and technical colleges. Her career has brought her into contact with many businesses both large and small, and she currently works for an international banking group. She is the author of *Climbing the Ladder: How to be a Woman Manager* and *How to be a Successful Business Woman: Working for Yourself*.

In addition, she ran for many years a specialised riding-equipment business. She started the Ladies' Side-Saddle Association in 1974 and held the chair for six years, during which time she travelled extensively to lecture and train other teachers.

She lives in Croydon with an investment consultant and a black cat, but hopes soon to move out into the country.

By the same author

Riding Side-Saddle (*with Val Francis*)
Running a Stables as a Business
The Right Horse: An Owners' and Buyers' Guide
Running a Tack-Shop as a Business
Climbing the Ladder: How to be a Woman Manager
How to be a Successful Business Woman:
   Working for Yourself

JANET W. MACDONALD

The Super Saleswoman

Methuen · Mandarin

A Mandarin Paperback

THE SUPER SALESWOMAN

First published in Great Britain 1988
by Methuen London
This edition published 1989
by Methuen · Mandarin
Michelin House, 81 Fulham Road, London SW3 6RB

Mandarin is an imprint of the Octopus Publishing Group

Copyright © 1988 by Janet W. Macdonald

British Library Cataloguing in Publication Data

Macdonald, Janet W, *1944–*
   The super saleswoman.
   1. Salesmanship – Manuals
I. Title
   658.8'5

   ISBN 0–7493–0022–1

Printed in Great Britain
by Cox & Wyman Ltd, Reading

For
Anne Brett, June Chisholm,
Mide Coker, Thea Nockels,
Ruth Pitsillides, Joyce Pohl,
Judy Tame – and all the others.

Contents

Introduction

Do you know the story of the thief who was asked by a prison visitor why he robbed banks? He looked pityingly at the visitor and said, 'Because that's where the money is!'

Robbing banks is not the most suitable career for women, and, contrary to popular supposition, it isn't actually that profitable. There aren't many careers that are, or not that are available to the average woman. But there is one, where you get paid on merit, not gender; where you need no formal qualifications to start; and where, as far as earnings are concerned, the sky is the limit.

I refer to selling. Not the retail situation, where you wait for customers to come to you, but real selling, where you go out and get them. Good salespeople are the lifeblood of any business, and they are eagerly sought by employers and rewarded in ways that reflect that importance. They don't care if the salesperson is male or female, all they care about is the orders coming in. In any organisation, the top sales team has praise and prizes heaped upon it, is given pride of place at the annual convention, and is as highly paid as any member of the board.

More and more frequently, these top teams are dominated by women. Women can often gain an appointment where a man cannot, and once in front of the customer can use her innate people-handling skills to win the order. For this reason, many companies are actively recruiting women for their sales teams.

Alas, I am not aware of any big organisation that runs separate selling skills courses for the women on its sales force. There is no sinister chauvinism in this; they just haven't realised that women have special problems that men don't, or that women have special skills that need to be nurtured and directed. (Guess which gender runs the sales training department in most big companies?) Alas again, although there are many hundreds of books on selling, or on specific aspects of selling, none of them are written for women. Which is why I have written this one, specifically for women who are, or who want to be, selling for a living.

The problems involved are those of women in any career, and I have already written of them in my books for women managers and women running their own businesses. I make no apology for doing so again in this book, for they are equally valid. The special skills have also been mentioned briefly in my other books, but are considerably expanded here, as they are central to the female ability to close a sale where a man might not.

It is stupid to try and pretend that men and women are equal and identical when it is patently obvious that we are not. Quite apart from the physical differences, our thought processes have evolved differently and women have developed their caring and nurturing roles to a stage where we often know intuitively how to handle strangers. And that skill is the most valuable you can have in the selling game.

When the stakes are high, the competition is legion and the customers are limited, there is only one rule that matters – if you've got an edge, use it. As a woman, you have that edge anyway. This book is to help you sharpen it.

Because using the cumbersome 'he or she' when referring to salespeople, customers and managers is unwieldy, I have used 'he' throughout, except when talking about the specific problems of selling to women. This is, thankfully, no longer a reflection of the true situation.

March 1988

1 Getting the job

Whether you are an experienced salesperson looking for new horizons or a rank beginner wanting to get into selling, it is worth developing a career plan rather than just seeking a new job now. This is one of the major areas that men in general are good at and women are not. Men plan their career, and each new job is a logical step towards their pre-planned goal; we think that maybe we should move on and look for a job we can do, and then wonder why we get left behind.

Even in such an equal-opportunity career as selling, the person who will reach the top of the heap is the one who has thought about how to get there. Where? Well, that's the first question you should ask yourself.

Is your prime objective making a lot of money, regardless of the product and selling methods? Or would you rather make a reasonable living selling an ethical product that lets you sleep at night? Are you sure your view of the product is based on logical facts? For instance, many people view life assurance salesmen as greedy charlatans, but the world is full of widows and orphans who have cause to be grateful for the policy their husband/father would not have bought without prompting from a salesman. Remember that air crash a few years ago that killed seven members of a parachute club from South Wales? That club had just been visited by a life assurance salesman and his company paid out on every one of those deaths, even though the policies hadn't yet been issued. I promise you, there is nothing unethical about life assurance.

On the other hand, consider double glazing. If you are listed in the phone book and you have not had at least six calls in the last year from people trying to sell you double glazing, you are lucky. It is often sold on the grounds that it will rapidly repay its cost by saving on heating bills, but the salespeople do not mention the additional cost of the finance interest, nor the loss of earnings on capital if you pay outright, nor do they produce independent proof of their cost-saving claims. If a minimum of five years is your idea of 'rapidly', it isn't mine. And don't you realise that thick curtains are just as effective in preventing heat loss? But many people are heavily pressurised into buying double glazing for no better reason than that the salesman wants his commission.

Do you have an interest in a particular specialised field? You may need qualifications for this. For instance, medical supply companies do require some evidence of technical know-how, whether it is a degree in chemistry or a nursing certificate. On the whole, it is only such very technical products that require formal qualifications, so if you do not have a technical bent there are still plenty of fields open to you. The bad news is that many of them only recruit people with sales experience.

If you have none, your first step is to find a company that will take you on as a trainee. Not only one that will take you on, but one that has a proper formal training programme for its trainees. 'On the job' training is not good enough. It usually consists of a bored manager who has not had any formal education in dealing with beginners, who will soon leave you to your own devices and wonder why you fall by the wayside.

A few more thoughts on career planning. Unless you are a masochist, do aim for industries that are sufficiently up to date to acknowledge that females can do other things besides type and make coffee. Any industry or company that makes a fuss about upholding tradition is likely to come into this category. There are other industries that are superficially forward-thinking, but still horrendously chauvinistic at grass-roots level. There are very few women selling to farmers, engineering companies, the building trade or heavy industry – not to mention the motor trade. Without exception, every car sales manager I spoke to when researching this book called me 'dear' and talked down to me, even when I mentioned that I had run a garage workshop for three years and done my share of the repair work.

The industries that welcome women with open arms include all those with female-oriented products like cosmetics; finance; business machines, services and supplies; hygiene services and medical products; publishing and advertising.

Do give some thought to whether your chosen industry will last as long as your career needs it to. The world is changing at an increasing rate, and products can reach saturation point (almost everyone has a deep-freeze now) or be superseded (I wonder how long compact discs will last?). There will always be a market for health care, beauty products, financial services and food, and we are told that there will be an increasing demand for leisure products and services. One can see that there is currently a growing market for retirement homes and home security systems, but will these be overtaken by changes in population and social attitudes? It's all worth thinking about.

Whilst your career strategy should involve moving jobs fairly regularly to gain experience and climb up your chosen ladder, don't do it too often. You should aim to stay at least two years in each job, or you will be branded a 'job-hopper'. Whoever the employer, they will be giving you product training if not sales training, and expect to recoup the costs from your sales. It pays to acquire some industry visibility outside your company (write letters to the trade press, join networks, blow your own trumpet at exhibitions and conferences), and you should never burn your bridges when you leave a job, no matter how great the provocation. Your ex-boss may also have industry visibility and lots of contacts. Or you may want to go back to that company one day and, even though your *bête noire* may have gone, he could have put an adverse report on your file.

If you want to get a start in selling and are looking for a job with a basic salary (and for trainees, this can be very 'basic' indeed!) there are only three possibilities. One is big household-name suppliers of FMCG (fast-moving consumer goods); the others are office equipment and life assurance. All are fully aware of the value of women in selling, and most have good training programmes.

Where office equipment is concerned there may be certain areas of physical limitation, but there is often a way round this. For instance, one of the better known photocopier companies has several different sales forces. It does not accept women to sell the machine to end-users, but does have women on the team that seeks new wholesalers. This team does not have to lug the machines into the customer's office for demonstrations, but invites the customer to the area office instead.

If you are prepared to accept a self-employed, commission-only job, and have a financial buffer behind you to see you through the lean months at the beginning, the scope is wider. Almost without exception these jobs are in 'direct' selling, which means 'direct to the public'. You will be selling home improvements (windows, kitchens, bathrooms etc.), self improvement (encyclopaedias, typing courses, typewriters), household effects (vacuum cleaners, cookware etc.), financial services or time shares.

A few words of warning about direct sales jobs. Do make sure that you will receive proper training. Reputable companies put you on a course as soon as you join them and you should not give in your notice to your current employer until you have a formal letter of acceptance with instructions about joining the course.

Do be sure that the deal you are being offered is the same one that everyone gets. There should be a proper printed contract, and a reasonable interviewer will let you discuss it with other people who work for them. (This does not apply if you have experience and can prove you are brilliant. Every sales manager will bend over backwards to recruit a top producer from a rival company. You may be able to negotiate a super-normal deal for yourself, with a golden hello, special car, volume bonuses, a personal assistant, and who knows what else; but don't hand in your notice until you have the offer in writing from head office. Your recruiter may have exceeded his authority and you'll end up with egg on your face.)

Make sure you know exactly how much you will be paid, and how, and when. If there are to be 'advances' or 'financing' or 'a monthly draw', find out if you have to repay these if you do not earn enough commission to cover them. Ask if any of your true earned commission (sometimes known as 'actuals', but meaning commission due on items you have actually sold) will be retained for any reason. Some less reputable companies retain what they call 'loyalty money' from each sale for several months and then won't let you have it if you leave.

Finally, do probe to be sure you know exactly who you are working for. Many direct sales jobs, especially in the home improvements field, are not with the company whose household name is above the door, but with a franchise. You will go to the named company for your training, and you may well be tied to selling their products only, but your contract will be with the franchisee. Such franchises have a nasty habit of going bust, and if that happens, you won't get paid.

There is one other reliable way of getting into real selling from the outside, and that is a telesales job. It will be a 'small basic plus commission' type salary, it should include training, and it consists of spending your working day on the telephone. You will either be making appointments for a salesperson, or actually trying to persuade people to buy a service (frequently advertisements in newspapers or magazines). Since nine out of ten people you phone will reply, 'No thank you,' firmly, or 'Push off, I'm busy,' or just put the phone down and walk off, leaving you with an open line you can't get away from, you will soon find out if you really do want to sell. If you are good at it, you can make quite a lot of money, and you have certainly demonstrated to your next employer that you can cope at the sharp end.

There are many recruitment agencies that specialise in sales jobs. Some only operate in one industry, but others are more general. All these agencies like women – one of the better known agencies told me that they were able to place a much higher percentage of female applicants than male. Just keep in mind that agencies are paid by the employers whose jobs they fill, not by the job-seeker (they are forbidden by the Employment Agencies Act to charge you a fee for finding you a job). They are looking for a round peg to fill a round hole and if you are a square peg, they will make polite noises, take your details and forget you. They can do nothing else, for they are, after all, in business to make money, and hawking square pegs about the market is not cost-effective for them.

There are companies that offer 'career assessment', training and help in obtaining a job. This involves teaching you to write an application letter, practising interviews (often with the help of video), and providing you with a beautiful CV. Unless they have a separate division that is a proper licensed employment agency, they will not be able to arrange interviews for you. Some of these organisations do try very hard to turn you out as a polished end product, but their sales training is, of necessity, generalised and thus rarely valued by specific industry employers. The courses offered by these companies are rather expensive, normally a four-figure sum. For a few hundred pounds you can obtain the same thing under the Phoenix programme, which is run at polytechnic colleges with the blessings of the Manpower Services Commission. See the Appendix for addresses.

So how do you get that first job if the agencies aren't interested in you? Via the usual methods, of course. If you have your heart set on a particular industry, write a short letter to all the big names saying you are thinking of a career change, and do they have a sales training programme? At the same time, start looking at job ads in the papers and the trade press (ask for lists of trade magazines at your local library), but read them with a big pinch of salt. If the same ad keeps appearing, ask yourself why they have to keep recruiting new people all the time – because they treat them badly and they move on, that's why.

Ignore all the ads that don't tell you what the company or the product is, no matter how exciting the job looks.

Some people don't answer the telephone with the company name, and won't tell you what the product is until you come to the 'seminar' – 'We don't want you coming with any preconceived ideas.' What they mean is that you wouldn't go near them if you knew who they were or what they were selling, and they want to expose you to mass hysteria. This is often the latest version of pyramid-selling, and the organisers want you to part with money in exchange for 'stock'.

You should also ignore the ads that offer 'a monkey and a jam-jar and a dog-and-bone' (do you really want to work with that sort of smart Alec?) or say: 'I used to be broke, but now I've got a house in Gerrards Cross and a Mercedes and I need someone to help me.' This last one has been running for several years now, with a multitude of names and telephone numbers – Gerrards Cross must be populated entirely by successful salespeople and their Mercedes! And ignore the ads that offer you '£20,000 plus OTE'. OTE means 'on-target earnings', or 'if you're not earning that by the end of the year, you're out'. It certainly does not mean you get that much automatically.

All these ads are for the grotty end of direct sales – the jobs you would hesitate to tell your friends about. They have to keep advertising in this underhand way because they have an enormous turnover of recruits and the sales managers who place the ads are under heavy pressure to get their numbers up. Some companies are even dumb enough to reward their managers for a net manpower gain rather than a production gain. So the manager only wants you there as a name on the board, and doesn't care much if you never sell anything. He certainly won't go out of his way to help you – he's too busy recruiting the next sucker!

The worst sort expect you to pay them for leads (in cash) or give them a share of your commission (in cash) as well as the override commission that is their proper earnings on your sales. They are not all like this, of course, but plenty are at that end of the market. If you are prepared to fight your way through that sort of world, fine, but if not, steer clear. Just keep in mind that their reason for recruiting you may not be the same as your reason for joining them.

Probably the best places to have a look at prospective employers are exhibitions. There are the specialised ones such as 'money' shows, where everyone in the financial services industry will have a stand, or 'business to business' shows, which cover everything from computers to personalised paperclips. These shows are staged by local Chambers of Commerce, as well as big exhibition organisers, so you will not have to go to London to attend, as you will with the Ideal Home Exhibition. This includes financial services, personal computers and all sorts of areas that you might not think relate to home improvement. Think 'lifestyle improvement', and you will soon see who might be there.

At these shows, you can look at several representatives of each industry in one day. You can see the quality and market-positioning of the products, and each company's sales approach, and weed out the ones that conflict with your inclinations. You will get a much better idea of each company than you would at an ordinary interview, you can talk to the salespeople and with luck get their unexpurgated version of what the job entails, rather than the official line. They will also tell you exactly who to contact if you want to carry on. The main element of selling is prospecting for customers, and this is exactly what you are doing – seeking a customer for your talents. You will impress a prospective boss by havng done this elementary homework before you ask for an interview.

The interview itself, and you may have a sequence of them with various levels of managers, will be a double-sided selling operation. They want to sell you the job, and you want to sell them yourself. It's hackneyed, but 'Sell yourself and you can sell anything' still holds true.

Sell yourself – don't give yourself away. Make sure you are clear about, and happy with, all the important aspects mentioned above – remuneration package, training, reporting structure. Don't forget to ask about leads. Some companies charge for them (officially), while some do not give them to trainees at all. This is not meanness. They have paid to generate them and they want them to go to salespeople who can be guaranteed to convert them to sales. Some, though not as many as used to, charge a deposit on the presentation kit. This is not unreasonable either, considering the cost of such kits, provided that the deposit is refunded when you return the kit on leaving. If not, ask yourself if their intention is to sell the product, or the presentation kits!

If you anticipate the major questions you may be asked, and have your answers ready, you will not be caught out if a little editing is called for. I am not suggesting you lie, but if the job is selling office supplies, 'I have six "O" levels, including Maths and Commerce' will do more for you than listing them all when the others are 'Cookery, Needlework, Basket-Weaving and Flower-Arranging'.

You will be caught out if you omit to tell the full truth about your credit status and job history. Few employers ask to see exam certificates for selling jobs, but many will be obtaining a 'fidelity bond' on you. This applies to all those jobs where you handle any form of money: either cash, cheques, direct debit mandates or applications for loans.

Being 'bonded' involves two areas. Bonding companies check your job history and do not like unexplained gaps between jobs, or discrepancies between the dates you give and the ones past employers give. Professional cynics, the bonding companies suspect that gaps in employment or education mean a spell in prison. Criminal convictions are not a matter of public record and so they cannot prove it either way, but they may well turn you down on the suspicion. If you were unemployed, give them the address of the DHSS office where you signed on, and a letter giving them permission to verify this. If you were travelling, offer your passport to prove it. If you were bumming around doing nothing for a while, offer respectable personal referees who can vouch for you. If you were in prison you have a problem, and I can only suggest that you try a different industry, one that does not seek bonding.

The other area bonding companies check is your credit status. This is nothing to do with the credit 'scoring' that card companies do before they give you a card. It involves checking that you do not have a history of debt, which might tempt you to do naughty things. There are a number of credit reference agencies, but the two main ones have computerised systems which subscribers can gain access to through Prestel. As well as bonding companies, subscribers will include credit granters and banks, and they provide information as well as ask for it. If you have ever defaulted on a loan, or been late with repayments, or have any County Court Judgements (CCJs) against you, it all shows on the computer, so don't be tempted to lie. You may not automatically be disbarred from the job if you do have CCJs, but few companies like liars. CCJs are not that uncommon these days, especially after a marriage break-up and if you tell them why the judgements occurred and prove that you are paying the debts off, all should be well.

If you are turned down for a job and can think of no reason why, it may just be that one of the credit reference agencies has got its facts wrong about you. Ask the personnel department which one they use (they are obliged to tell you under the Data Protection Act) and then write to that agency and ask for a copy of your file. They are obliged to give it to you, and also to correct it if it is wrong.

Something that a lot of big companies are doing now with potential recruits is psychometric testing, or bio-data and attitude testing. Even if you have been selling successfully for years, they will still insist that you do the tests for statistical purposes. Psychometric and attitude tests are intended to produce a 'personality profile' of you, which is meant to indicate whether you are suitable for a selling career. Bio-data tests (bio-data means biographical data, i.e. your life/job history and current situation) will be checked against statistical data for the same purpose.

You cannot always tell what sort of test is being carried out, although if it is dominated by lists of word groups where you mark what is most and least like you, it is a personality test. The people who devise these tests sell them on the basis that they cannot be faked, and that they are highly predictive of the candidate's suitability for the job. Occupational psychologists say that a lot more work needs to be done on them, and many user companies say they feel they are a useful tool but would not rely on them entirely.

The problem is that there is no arguing with the results. Many of the tests go to an independent marking bureau who will tell the employers no more than 'Yes', 'No' or 'Maybe', and then destroy the test paper. They won't tell you anything. The Phoenix programme includes some of these tests, and they do discuss the results with you, so if you are being turned down consistently after doing these tests it might be worth investigating.

Incidentally, 'No' or a cool 'Maybe' doesn't necessarily mean that you aren't cut out for selling at all. There are reckoned to be at least nine distinct types of salesperson, ranging from 'missionary goodwill builder' to 'creative technical specialist'. You might be one sort, when the test is designed to select only another sort, so keep trying. If *you* are convinced you can sell, don't let a mere psychometric test change your mind.

2 Dress for results

If 'sell yourself' is the first rule of selling, the second must be 'package the product properly' – and the package is you. Whether it is for a job interview or a sales presentation, the initial picture you present is the one that impresses and the one by which you will be judged. It is up to you to ensure that the image you project is what you want it to be.

Your appearance is a major contributor to your credibility with your customers. Assuming that it is not your body that is for sale, the picture you should present is of a competent, confident, businesswoman, not a frivolous scatterbrain or a smouldering seductress.

You cannot force your customers to buy your product, whatever it is. You can only advise them to do so, which means that you should dress like the people they usually go to for advice they respect – lawyers, accountants, bank managers. In other words, dress conservatively. This doesn't mean that you shouldn't dress well. Nobody wants to do business with a loser, so the overall impression should be of affluence. (That rule applies to cars as well. If you do not have a company car, buy the best quality car you can. For the price of a two-year-old mid-range Ford, you can get a six-year-old Mercedes or Volvo that will be just as reliable and cost no more to run. If you are worried about the registration letter prefix giving you away, invest a few hundred more pounds in a 'cherished' registration number.)

Large companies usually prefer to deal with outsiders who look like their own executives. If you are not sure what that means, lurk outside their offices and have a look. The more serious their business, the darker their executive suits will be, and the less likely they are to relax into paler colours in summer. If you want them to take you seriously as an equal, you must do the same. You also have to get past their 'gatekeepers' (receptionists, secretaries, etc.) who will assume that you have low status unless you dress like the people they know to have authority.

Black may be a little extreme unless you are selling to lawyers, but you won't go far wrong in mid- to dark-blue or grey two-piece suits or dresses. In less formal situations, you might go for darkish reds, browns, greens or camel. If you don't like plain colours, go for tweeds, flecks or discreet repetitive patterns rather than bold splashes of pattern. Suits are best with a matching jacket rather than 'mix and match', and the jacket should be classically cut. You should not take off your jacket, no matter how hot it may be, even if your customer invites you to.

Blouses or shirts should be neither fussy, frilly, nor low-cut. The neck can be shirt-collared, stand-up or tied in a bow. Men's shirts are perfectly acceptable and cost about a third of the price of women's shirts and blouses. You can always dress up the neckline or provide some colour by adding a scarf, but never, never a man's tie. Men don't like it, and women think you're butch. A combination of skirt and blouse or woolly jumper is not a good idea. Even if you do not have to keep tucking yourself in at the waist, they suggest the typing pool rather than the executive. If you do not like suits, it is better to choose a dress.

Dresses should also be businesslike. They should not be low-cut, clingy or skimpy. You arms should be covered.

Neither dresses nor suits should be extravagantly waisted, but padded shoulders are fine so long as they are not too extreme. If you are small, they add to your size and thus your authority, as does a tailored, even military, look.

Whatever you wear, it must fit properly. People assume that sloppy dress means a sloppy mind, and they won't let you stay around long enough to prove that handsome is as handsome does. If buttons are straining, diet or buy a bigger size. If clothes are too big, or loose where they shouldn't be, find someone to make alterations for you. Choose a skirt length you like (preferably long enough to cover your knees when you sit) and stick to it, instead of playing yo-yo hems when the fashion world demands. If you elect to wear men's shirts, get tucks put in them to accommodate your bust.

Even if your bust is small, *never* go without a good bra. Jiggly breasts and protruding nipples embarrass most men, but some will interpret them as a sign that you fancy them. Nipples erect automatically when you are excited or tense, either of which can happen in a selling situation.

If you prefer stockings to tights, be sure that your suspenders do not show through your skirt. They may also be interpreted as a come-on. And don't cross your legs when you sit facing a man. You will inevitably want to uncross them or recross them the other way, and he may think you are trying to show him your thighs.

If you behave, or dress, in what could be interpreted as a sexy manner, you will be treated as a sex object rather than a businesswoman – which is precisely what the fashion industry is all about. It promotes the idea that clothes are for man-catching and that only the latest fad will do that. Since it wants to sell a lot of clothes, it produces new fads every year and tries to blackmail you into buying them. Even if you are in the fashion industry yourself, you should avoid the sexy extremes of see-through fabrics, leather trousers or cripplingly tight skirts. You are there to *sell* the product, not model it.

If you are not in the fashion industry, steer clear of fads or you risk being thought lightweight. Faddy clothes are also frequently shoddy. They crease easily, don't hang right and soon look tired, giving the impression of sloppiness. Don't forget that you will be spending much of your working day getting in and out of cars or public transport, going into a series of customer's premises that may not be that clean, maybe carrying a presentation kit and bending or stretching while you make that presentation.

So choose garments that do not pick up dirt or fluff, and that fall back into place on their own. That means classic lines, good cut and good quality fabrics. If you do not feel confident about choosing these for yourself, get professional help. There are independent 'wardrobe engineers' or 'image consultants' who advertise in the better monthly magazines. They will come to your home, assess your current wardrobe, then help you draw up a plan and even go shopping with you, all for an hourly fee. Some of them may also be 'seasonal colour consultants' who decide that you have a 'spring' (or whatever) personality and give you specific colours to buy. This is all right as long as they don't major on those pale colours you should avoid.

Good-quality clothes are not cheap, and this is one of the reasons why you should go for classic lines. If you pay a lot for your clothes, you should be able to wear them for a long time, which brings down the cost per wearing. If you are not already aware of that concept, get it firmly into your head now. Do the arithmetic on each item before you buy it. Take the price, add the price of any accessories it needs that won't go with anything else you own, then ask yourself how often you will want to wear it and how often it will have to be cleaned. Add the cost of two years' cleaning bills to your previous total, then divide the new total by the number of times you will wear it in that two years. If the cost per wearing is more than 5 per cent of your weekly income for one outfit, don't buy it. If it is less, and it still looks good after two years, you are on free time.

Once you have a good basic wardrobe, it will be relatively inexpensive to maintain, but you will have to be prepared to spend quite a lot of money at the start. Even if you decide to wear nothing but suits and shirts, you will need at least two suits, for even the best of fabrics needs to rest for a day between wearings if it is to retain its shape. This is why you need a definite wardrobe plan. If you know you need a specific item, you can look for it during the sales, when it won't cost so much. And if you find a particular manufacturer whose styles you like, you can buy their clothes in smaller towns instead of having to go to big cities where the prices are inflated to cover city costs.

There is another way to buy good clothes at bargain prices if you're broke and don't have false pride. Go to a quality second-hand clothes shop (they are listed in the *Yellow Pages* as 'dress agencies'). There are several very reputable long-established ones in London. They often have items that have never been worn, sent in by the sort of woman with more money than sense who goes on buying sprees. Even the clothes that have been worn are in immaculate condition. The agencies will not accept them otherwise.

The affluent, professional image you want to create

means an upper-middle-class look, and that means natural fabrics: wool, cotton, linen or silk rather than nylon; leather rather than plastic. But never fur. Synthetic 'fur', despite manufacturers' claims, very quickly looks tatty and downmarket. And real fur, however one may dislike the emotionalism that has caused it, is offensive to a lot of people. If you wear it to an organisation that proclaims its orientation, like Greenpeace, you're asking for trouble; and if you wear it anywhere else, you might be shown the door without ever knowing why.

Your own hair should be under control. Long hair is reckoned to be sexy, so keep yours no more than shoulder length, or pin it up. Add to your height, if you are short, by piling it on top of your head. If you feel the need for colouring, have it done professionally and often enough to stop it showing at the roots. Don't comb it in front of customers nor fiddle with it. That is either done deliberately to be provocative, or unconsciously as what zoologists call 'displacement behaviour' – a 'got to do something with my hands' response to embarrassment or uncertainty.

Don't let floppy hair or fringes obscure your face. Your face is an important part of your communication equipment and you do not want anything to impede it in that function. These impediments include unusual features which draw and hold the observer's attention to the exclusion of everything else. I'm not suggesting major plastic surgery, but large moles are easily removed and uneven or bad teeth are easily dealt with by a competent dentist.

If you've got dark hairs on your chin, get some tweezers and pull the damn things out. It's the only way. Electrolysis is not the instant cure the ads would like you to believe – you have to go every fortnight for at least a year. And they can't electrolyse a hair they can't see, so you have to let them grow long, and quite often your skin objects to the needle and presents you with a pimple. So you spend your life being alternately hairy or spotty, neither of which does anything for your confidence. (If you get lots of spots anyway, it's time you altered your eating habits.)

Don't obscure your eyes with dark glasses – people think you have something to hide if they can't see your eyes. Ordinary spectacles are fine; they can even be a help if you feel that a little extra authority is called for, and you can take them off and gesture with them to gain time when awkward questions are asked. If you don't need them for sight correction but want a pair for the other reasons, do have plain lenses in the frames, rather than empty frames. Sod's law says you will get an itchy eyelid and give yourself away by poking a finger in to scratch! And don't take your glasses off and put the sidepieces in your mouth. That oral display will put male observers into quite the wrong state of mind!

Make-up should be low-key, but you will need some. Office lighting tends to drain colour from the face and make you look haggard. Do it properly before you leave home, then all you need do during the day is to check for shiny nose and wan lips before you go in to each appointment. If you are using public transport you may need to do a little more than powder your nose, but try to avoid retiring to a customer's toilet for a full re-paint job. Female staff are bound to see you and may make a derogatory comment to your buyer.

As with clothes, cheap make-up does not wear well, so buy the best you can. The same goes for perfume. The cheap sort either disappears quickly altogether, or parts of it fade and leave an unfortunate residue. Better to wear none than that. Go for light scents or colognes and leave the heady musky ones for your evenings out.

I don't need to tell you about deodorants, do I?

Jewellery should be kept to a minimum, too. Choose a simple brooch or necklace and a classic watch with a simple strap. Silver or gold offends nobody, but junk jewellery is frivolous and masses of chains or bangles that rattle are a distraction. Sparklers are for evening wear, or engagement rings.

Grubby hands and nails are dreadful. If you are a painter or gardener, wear gloves for your hobby or scrub harder in the bath. Keep your nails well manicured, not too long, and not too bright. Clear polish, if you must use any, at least does not show chips. Many people think unpolished nails are more businesslike.

More and more people these days consider smoking to be a disgusting habit, so watch out for nicotine stains on your hands. And for heaven's sake, don't smoke in customer's offices. You're there to do a job, not indulge your habits or soothe your nerves. Don't smoke in their toilets, either. We had a visitor to our office who used to smoke in the Ladies, ignoring the sign on the door. She'd leave a cigarette burning on the tiles until it left a nasty brown stain, or you'd find the remains floating in the loo. To this day, she is referred to as 'Fag-ash Lil'.

In winter you will need gloves – proper leather ones (without fur linings). Avoid black, as it is associated with mourning. Natural browns or tan are always accept-able; navy or grey go with most other colours. Knitted gloves or mittens are for little girls, and fabric gloves are downmarket, as are plastic.

Much the same applies to shoes. Medium-height plain pumps go with most outfits, and will allow you to walk reasonable distances without hurting your feet. Teetery heels restrict your freedom of movement, besides being sexy. Boots should be kept for really bad weather and even then should not be fashionably extreme. Patent leather looks beautiful when it is new, but tends to crack after a while. Suede marks, as does fabric, and plastic is cheap and nasty, so plain leather is best. If you are driving, don't drive in your business shoes or the heels will soon mark. And whatever shoes you choose, keep them in good repair and *clean*. It is amazing how many people (men too) ruin their appearance with scruffy shoes.

Don't take any notice of fashion diktats about matching shoes and handbag – what they want is your money. What you want is a briefcase and a slim clutch bag that fits in it to hold your make-up and cash. There's no reason why your briefcase should be black, as long as it is businesslike and not gimmicky. It's safest to choose one with combination locks and keep it locked, then there's no chance of it falling open and spilling things. Keep the little handbag in it, or you'll spoil the executive image.

Keep a couple of respectable pens handy, in case of need. 'Can't find my pen,' is a standard excuse for buyers who want to stall, and it gives you the upper hand to produce a good stylish pen for signing. You certainly should not give them an excuse to look down their nose at you by offering them a cheap chewed ballpoint.

For winter, you will need a good warm coat, and for wet days a good raincoat. And I do mean a coat, not a poncho or cloak or shawl, and it should preferably be tailored. In the winter, if you feel the cold, add layers of underwear (thermal if you are a really chilly mortal) rather than woollies. Sweaters spell secretary.

Like everything else, hats should be understated rather than dramatic. No big brims, floppy brims, veils or pillboxes. Headscarves are tricky – little ones imply obscure religious sects, while big silk ones say 'Sloane Ranger', which may not be appropriate. You'll have to judge that one for yourself. You don't have to wear anything on your head, but if you do, take it off when you go into people's offices.

If you like an umbrella in wet weather, make it a good big one that really keeps the rain off all of you. If your company produces umbrellas with its logo superimposed, carry spares in your car for customers who admire yours. They cost very little for the goodwill which that gesture brings.

All the above may sound rather dictatorial, but it is a good base to start from. Once you have carved yourself a niche in a particular marketplace, you can judge whether to modify your style to fit your customers. The 'upmarket' image will never let you down in big cities, but it might overwhelm small-town people a little. Just look at the men – dark suits mean dark colours for you; tweed jackets mean you can relax a little, as long as you don't relax so far as to turn yourself out like 'the little woman'. Pink or lavender or pale blue in large quantities are *out*, even in the provinces.

If you are going to travel long-distance for your company, think a little more carefully about your clothes. There is not a lot of difference between the UK and northern Europe, but attitudes change as you go further south or east. If in doubt, ask senior women or senior secretaries who have travelled for your company for their advice, or take the trouble to get copies of women's magazines from those countries. 'Cover up' is not a bad rule to follow, and you may need to modify your behaviour styles as well, especially in Moslem countries.

America and Canada are easier, for they have similar cultures to our own, but it is a big continent, and mores do change as you travel across. In the North-East (New York, Boston, Washington) and certain other big cities (Los Angeles and San Francisco in the West, Dallas and Atlanta in the South) you will be fine in your London clothes. In the Mid-West, they are not too keen on 'pushy Easterners', so you need to soften a little, but still stay conservative. In the South, they are not too keen on outsiders at all, they think women should be women and they prefer Southern women to any other sort.

If you have to go down there, slow down your speech (the damn Yankees are fast-talkers), don't let them see you drinking alcohol, and don't wear anything that could remotely be construed as masculine. Don't wear black, which is masculine, but neither should you wear pink, lilac or gold, which were traditionally chosen by the other sort of working girl in New Orleans!

As to the actual travelling, pack a change of clothes and your make-up into the bag you carry with you on the plane. Then you won't be in trouble if the airline loses your luggage. Unpack as soon as you get to your hotel and give anything that is not pristine to the valet service.

Hotels are gradually getting the message about businesswomen travellers, but don't hesitate to make a dignified fuss if your room is not suitable or lacks what you need. If you hand over a business card when you check in, they have no excuse for mistaking you for a hooker, and they won't want adverse reports preventing your company from using them again.

And wherever you are at home or abroad, remember that everyone you encounter could be a customer. You must always be 'on parade'.

3 Reading people

Once you have accepted that you should be dressing in a way that makes deliberate statements about you, it is a small step to realising that the way your customers dress can tell you a lot about them.

Rule One is that powerful people are always turned out immaculately. This is a throwback to the days when only the rich could afford lots of clothes. So it is a reasonable assumption that any customer who is beautifully dressed has a fair bit of clout. It may also follow that the scruffy ones don't, but don't make the mistake of assuming that people with upper-crust accents who wear old clothes are totally unimportant. Look again and you will see that, old though the clothes may be, they are top quality; you have just encountered aristocratic thrift and style. Nor does it follow that you should be offhand with the scruffy. Unimportant they may be, but they might also be your only route to the person who does have the purchasing power. You need all the allies you can get in the 'enemy' camp.

Business people all wear some sort of 'uniform'. With big organisations, you will learn to judge the value of suits and other trappings, but in smaller companies, particularly manufacturers, the boss may be almost indistinguishable from the factory workers. And the receptionist-cum-tea-lady may be his wife, so be charming to everybody. Even if you are present when the boss reprimands someone, you should not join in or make derogatory comments about that person later. Useless he may be, but he belongs to the boss, who will feel obliged to defend him – against you!

When you are selling to customers in their own homes, it is easier to learn about them from their clothes and environment. If this seems to conflict with the people themselves, do ask, 'Have you been here long?' If they've just moved in, it is easy to comment on the traumas of redecorating, and they will soon tell you who chose the colour scheme and furniture. That should tell you who makes the purchasing decisions.

If the house is all rather too perfect, and the wife is also too perfect, the lady may be an obsessive nit-picker. If a couple's clothes, hair and décor are in the latest style, but the décor is marred by dirt or downmarket touches, it is a fair bet that they have come up in the world suddenly and are a little uncertain of their social position. With younger people of this type, it may have taken a lot of credit to achieve the trappings. You may not think that that aspect is your concern, but you do not want to bring in too many customers who default on payments.

With unashamedly scruffy houses you will be dealing with much more secure people who don't need to dress up their environment, but even they will regard their home as their territory and you must be careful that you do not constitute an 'invasion'.

The easiest way to do this inadvertently is to pick the wrong place to sit. Whether it is an easy chair or at a table, if you are not offered a specific place to sit, do ask, 'Where would you like me?' or 'Which is your chair?' If you choose the head of the house's chair, he will become agitated and defensive and more concerned with getting rid of you than listening to you. The worst possible place to sit is at the 'head' of the dining table. You can't always tell where this is with a round table, but it will probably be facing the door. If the dining space would allow any shape of table and they have chosen a rectangular one, they probably do place importance on seating.

With easy chairs, don't choose one that puts you in a higher position than them, as this might make them uneasy. On the other hand, beware of settees that drag you down into their depths, and where you have nowhere to put your briefcase. My fiancé tells a horror story of one such settee which was occupied by him, his briefcase and the family spaniel. No one noticed the intruding ear until he shut his briefcase firmly and trapped it! (Incidentally, if you are allergic to animals, don't make a fuss about it. Either put up with them, or find something to sell that doesn't involve going into people's homes. The same applies if you are a non-smoker or detest children.)

Seating arrangements in offices are a minefield of power ploys and territorial statements. You don't always have a choice about where to sit, but you can get an indication of how to behave from the way the furniture is arranged. It is a basic human reaction to place yourself in a defensive position with your back to a wall, and to feel uneasy if your back is exposed. It is a deliberate statement of superiority to arrange one's office so that visitors are in undefensible open spaces, so beware when you encounter this. Many professional buyers do it specifically to put salespeople at a disadvantage.

They do other things, too – like having a very big desk with its 'furniture' (ashtrays, telephones, etc.) arranged to leave you very little room; or taking off their watch and putting it face up on the desk, making it quite clear that your time is limited; or sitting with their back to the window so you have to squint into the bright light; or doing nasty things with chairs. They will have a big chair with a high back and arms (like a throne – only important people have thrones), and you will have to sit on a soft sofa which you fall back into, or on a small low chair, or on a chair with short front legs that tips you off balance, or on a heavy chair that is miles'away from their desk and which you can't move.

If you have a choice of chairs, or can move one, sit close to the desk but towards one corner. Not on the end – that's encroaching on his territory unless he gives permission either verbally or by gesture. Certainly you must not go round alongside him until he invites you or makes it sufficiently clear that he is very interested in the product. Then you say 'May I come round? I'd like to show you . . .'

If you have no option but to sit opposite him, be careful of moving his stuff on the desk to make room for yours. If he's interested, he'll move it himself. If the desk is empty, you may assume rights to the space on your side, but don't put things over the centre line – not even the things you are trying to show him. These you place on the centre line and wait to see what happens. If he leans forward to look at them, he will listen to what you have to say, but it had better be good. If he picks them up and takes them into his territory, he's interested, and you might think of getting closer yourself. But if he pushes them back to your side and leans back, he doesn't want to know. Have one more try to interest him, and if that doesn't work, give up and go while your dignity is still intact.

The other situation that is becoming more common is the office that has a desk for working and a round table for meetings. It's part of the 'standard manager's office package' sold by office furnishers, and about the only thing you can tell from it for sure is that you're in trouble if your 'host' doesn't sit at it. If he waves you to a specific chair, you can spread your stuff out on that bit of table once you've seen where he's going to sit. If he doesn't offer you a specific seat, try to avoid the 'back to the door' or 'back to the glass wall into the main office' seat, but don't put yourself on the side of the table nearest his desk unless you're sure he's staying at that desk.

The problem with people who don't come out from their desk is not only that they are in a territorial position that you should not encroach on, but that much of their body is hidden from you and you can't see all their body language. 'Body language' is one of those phrases that people use as if we all know about it, but unless you have studied it you will not be consciously aware of all the nuances. The ability to read body language, and to control your own, is one of the major sales skills you must perfect if you are to be successful.

As a woman, you will already recognise most of the courtship signals given by men and may also be sufficiently aware of the female courtship signals to use them yourself deliberately. Both sexes use 'preening' gestures like smoothing the clothes or hair, and both use gestures intended to display the crotch area. Men spread their legs or hook their thumbs in their belt so their hands point at their genitals. Women waggle their hips when they walk, cross and uncross their legs to display their thighs; and also use sideways glances, open their mouths, lick their lips, expose their wrists and palms (a surrender gesture) or suggest intercourse by thrusting a foot in and out of a shoe or fondling a convenient cylindrical object – wine-glass stem, pencil, cigarette.

I'm sure you won't be silly enough to do any of that when you are trying to sell your employer's product. But do you do it when you are with a man you fancy? Deliberately, or have you only now realised that all those little gestures you see or use yourself are part of standard body language? And of course, body language is not just confined to courtship. People use it all the time, adopting attitudes without realising they are doing it, but saying volumes to the educated observer. Like any language, it consists of words which can be put together to emphasise the statement; and it also uses words in different contexts to mean different things. Crossed legs and arms might mean 'I don't like you' or they might mean 'I'd love to listen to you, but I'm busting for a pee'! Only experience will tell you which is which.

The basic concept is that body language is about personal territory. We all like to have our personal space round us, and will take steps to maintain what is known as our 'acceptance distance'. This can lead to difficulties when we meet foreigners, as acceptance distances differ from country to country. The Japanese, for example, with their very crowded country, maintain their territory by extreme formality but stand very close compared with the British. City people, again because they are used to living in crowded conditions, stand closer than country people. So the city man puts himself at his usual distance from the country man, who feels uncomfortable and takes a step back. But the city man now feels too far away and steps forward . . . This can go on for some time until the country man ends up against a wall or can think of an excuse to get away.

We all have a series of zones around us, depending on how well we know, or want to know, the other person. The closest is the 'intimate' zone, which is for close family and lovers only. Next is the 'personal' zone, for friends and people at social gatherings. Our 'social' zone, usually more than four feet, is for the casual acquaintances we have to do business with. Finally we have a 'public' zone for total strangers.

If people get too close, we can back off, but that is a gesture of surrender and we don't want to do that on our own territory. What we do instead is adopt gestures of withdrawal or defensiveness. If you don't learn when your customer is withdrawing from you and do something about it, you will end an awful lot of interviews with your tail between your legs.

The most basic form of withdrawal is to lean back. In other words, to try to increase the distance between you without surrendering by moving the feet. It means, quite simply, 'I don't like you very much and I don't want you close.' It is emphasised, or sometimes replaced, by barriers made with the legs or arms. Legs are crossed, either standing or sitting, and the extremely nervous will double the gesture by twining them to cross again. Arm-crossing can be simple, or compounded by the hands gripping the upper arms in extreme anxiety, or by the hands clenched into fists in hostility. Some people don't actually cross their arms across their chest but will hold their own hands for security or hold something with both hands. Women may clutch their handbag in front of them; men may pull at their shirt cuffs or fiddle with their watch. It all means the same thing and you should back off to reassure them.

The opposite also applies. The person who likes you or is interested in what you are saying will open their body to you by opening their arms (putting elbows on knees or desk) or invite you into a closer zone by leaning towards you. You can then lean towards them, or move your chair a little closer.

Watch the attitude of the head. Up is neutral, tilted sideways means interest and down with the chin tucked in is negative (defending the throat). If you do a lot of presentations to large groups, you'll need to be prepared to get them involved at the beginning to break the 'heads down, arms folded, waiting to be bored' syndrome.

If, in addition to the chin being down, it is supported by the the thumb, with the index finger up the cheek and the other fingers over the mouth, what you are saying is being evaluated unfavourably. An excuse will be made, not an accusation, as mouth-covering is a universal gesture to cover up a lie. Children do it with two hands, adults with one, often disguising it with coughing, but both do it not only when they are lying but when they think you are. If your audience does it when you are speaking, it is your cue to stop and ask, 'Would you like to comment on that?' or say, 'Perhaps I should qualify that a little.'

There are a whole collection of gestures which people use when they are lying to you. They will touch their nose, which is a variation of trying to hide the offending mouth, rub an eye or an ear, scratch their neck or pull at their collar, blink very fast, blush or even break out into a sweat. Even the experienced professional liar may give himself away by involuntary expansion and contraction of the pupils.

The eyes are a great giveaway. The pupils dilate automatically when interest is raised, and wide pupils are one of the main signals of sexual attraction. It is one of the reasons why buyers situate their desks so that you are semi-blinded by having to look into the light and thus can't see their eyes. And of course, since they are looking into a darker area, their pupils will already be dilated, so it is difficult to gauge their reaction to your presentation.

Conversely, constricted pupils, assuming that they are not looking into the light, mean hostility. I used to know a night-club bouncer, a very nice man really, but he could produce these 'snake eyes' at will – and it was really quite frightening. But it certainly helped him in his job! If you see it in customers, it is time to back off. And if they look at you and produce long blinks, with the eyes deliberately shut, they are trying to tell you they're bored.

You can use the 'wide eyes' routine to your advantage, especially if you are able to rub your hands at the same time. Fast hand-rubbing means you have something really exciting, so you do that, tilt your head, open your eyes wide and smile. If the buyer does the same, he's in the bag. If he's not quite convinced, he'll stall and you'll have to try again. He might do it verbally, or with his spectacles, either chewing the sidepieces or cleaning the lenses. If he follows that by folding them up and putting them away, you've lost the battle, but if he puts them back on, you've got another chance.

Smokers have the perfect prop for stalling. It is a form of displacement behaviour, allowing them to go through their favoured ritual instead of having to make a decision. Pipe-smokers can play for ages, reaming and filling and tamping and sucking and chewing on the stem while they pretend to deliberate. But cigarette-smokers can tap off ash, or flick it, or blow smoke signals. Smoke blown up means they're feeling confident and positive, blown down means they're feeling suspicious and negative, and the faster they blow it, the more strongly they feel.

Your only chance is to interrupt the ritual somehow. But watch for the smoker who suddenly decides to stub out the cigarette before he's smoked his usual amount. He's decided he's had enough and, unless you act swiftly to take control, he'll end the conversation and show you the door.

There is a lot more, and you may find that some of the interpretations given here do not quite tally with what you have observed. Verbal language also varies from place to place – try asking an American for a rubber. It means contraceptive over there, while the item you want is known as an eraser. Now that you are aware of the possibilities, you will soon learn to interpret the body language of the people in your chosen socio-economic group.

One area in particular that will tell you a lot about people is one that I have already mentioned – displacement behaviour. It can consist of almost any action or series of actions, but it denotes ill-ease – either nervousness or embarrassment. It usually involves a pretence, like the eye-rubbing that allows a liar to look away from you, or the nervous cough that allows him to cover his mouth, and it usually indicates that you have hit a raw nerve. To police interrogators, it means that they are on the right track and should pursue that line of questioning, but in a selling situation it should warn you off. If you persist in making your customers uncomfortable they will soon find an excuse to get rid of you, and it won't be by buying something.

There is one situation where you may be able to turn this to your advantage. A sequence of suddenly arrested hand movements that are turned into another set of movements often denotes an attempt to give up smoking. Each smoker has a specific ritual behaviour 'loop' that they follow, as though their actions were on a pre-recorded loop of tape that instructs the muscles to move in a set way. Watch anyone you know who smokes and you will soon see that they always follow the same routine – hand to the place where the packet is stored (always the same place); ditto the lighter; open the packet in the same way; take out a cigarette and place it in mouth in the same way; apply flame and take exactly the same length of suck; expel the first mouthful of smoke – and so on.

I have already mentioned that you can take advantage of the momentary disorientation you cause if you interrupt the ritual. But the same disorientation occurs if the smoker interrupts the ritual himself by remembering that he's not meant to do it. He then feels embarrassed at being caught out and pretends he was going to do something else.

If you think this is what you are witnessing, ask, 'Have you given up smoking?' (not 'Are you trying to', which implies that you think he will fail in the attempt). If he says Yes, you can 'give him permission' for having started the set of movements by sympathising, then make him feel good by praising his courage and determination in giving up. If you can make him feel good about himself, he'll feel good about you, and that is just what you want.

4 Establishing rapport

Selling is principally about making people like you. 'Sell yourself' – remember? You could have the most marvellous product in the world, but if your prospect has taken a dislike to you, he will not buy from you at any price. So your task is to make him like you. As we have already seen, part of this involves respecting the invisible barriers he sets round his personal space, but that is rather negative. So what positive action can you take to get an invitation into that space, to become friends for long enough to turn him from a prospect into a customer?

It is called establishing rapport and consists, basically, of making him think that you are a kindred spirit. For the period of the sales interview, you have got to become like your prospect. If that sounds to you like a good way to end up confused about who you really are, don't worry. Since the techniques involved are based on copying the person you are with at the time, you will find that you revert to your normal persona when you leave them.

Just like the chameleon, which takes on the colour of the vegetation it sits on, you will soon learn to detect the character 'colouration' of your customers, and adapt to it. All it requires is that you observe people much more carefully and in slightly different ways than before.

The first technique is called 'mirroring' or 'carbon-copying'. It consists of duplicating the postures and gestures of the person you are with. You see it in long-married couples. They both move in the same way, as if they were twins. They rarely realise they are doing it, but you will be doing it deliberately but oh so subtly. If you are clumsy and obvious about it, your subject will think you are taking the mickey.

This can have its uses, especially if your customer brings in a 'technical expert' against you. These experts tend to adopt superiority gestures, to put you in your place, such as leaning back with their hands behind their head. If you do the same very obviously, they will become so disconcerted that they will change their position, usually adding some form of displacement behaviour. That puts you back in control of the interview.

Normally, though, you do not want people to realise that you are copying them, so you must shift your position gradually, or make it part of some legitimate movement such as handing over papers. He puts his hand behind his ear and leans that elbow on the wall – you find an errant strand of hair and tuck it behind your ear and leave your hand there for a while. If you are both standing and he has all his weight on one foot, you turn round to put down some papers and shift your weight as you turn back.

Where your subject has a specific movement that he performs repeatedly, you will need to find another movement that you can make in the same rhythm. He scratches his chin, you rub your ear. He taps his pencil on the desk, you tap your foot.

When you are selling to couples in their home, you need to be even more subtle, as it is more likely that one of them will notice and wonder what you are doing. But you should keep a close eye on them, to see what mirrored movements they do and who instigates the movement. Regardless of who is doing the talking, it is usually the one who initiates the movements who is the main decision-maker, and who should not be left out of your presentation.

The next stage of mirroring is matching breathing. Most people have their own favoured speed of breathing and get agitated if others in their close vicinity are obviously breathing at a different rate. As a general rule, slow breathing means calmness, and fast breathing means excitement. You can actually change your prospect's state of mind if you can change his rate of breathing.

You will probably want him calm during the first part of your presentation, accepting what you are saying without alarm. But as you get to the end, you want to raise his interest and get him keen and excited about the product. During your preliminary chat, watch his shoulders go up and down to establish his breathing rate, then gradually bring your own breathing to that speed. Make a break in the proceedings by taking a deep breath, expelling the air fairly noisily, then gradually change the speed at which you breathe. You may need to make pauses in what you are saying to take deep breaths again before he will follow you, but once you have established the lead in breathing speed, you can change it and he will change with you. Even if you do not actually want to change the breathing rate, your prospect will find it very comforting if you adopt his speed. He will lose his distrust of you as a stranger and be much more ready to listen to what you have to say.

The next place to seek a match is in voices. Voices can be high- or low-pitched, loud or soft, varied or monotonous, and the speech itself can be fast or slow and with or without pauses. Obviously you cannot expect to make your voice as low as a man's, but if your normal speech is very high-pitched you can, and should, bring it down to a lower pitch. If it is high to start with, it will inevitably get higher when you get excited. It will probably speed up, too, and your listeners will think you are getting hysterical. Men especially hate what they call 'shrill' or 'screeching' women.

Think of any of the Mark One silly bitches portrayed in situation comedy on television. They all speak very fast and very high, but if you see the actresses on chat shows, you will find that their normal speech is much slower and lower. Get someone to tape you and listen to see whether you should do something about your voice. It isn't that difficult, just a matter of training your vocal chords with a humming exercise.

Stand up straight and hum down the scale until you can't go any lower. Hold that note as long as you can. Do this four or five times a day and you will soon find you can get lower on the scale and that your normal speaking voice will drop down the scale as well. Your voice will go down, but your crediblity will go up.

You should not try to make sudden changes of pitch when you are talking to customers, but you should alter your volume and speed. People who normally talk slowly hate 'gabblers' and vice versa. It is another reason for the traditional distrust between city folk and country folk. What with 'fast-talking city slickers' on one side, and 'dumb hicks' on the other, it is little wonder that they look sideways at each other. Slow talkers also tend to be quiet talkers. Have you noticed that when someone whispers, everyone around goes quiet and strains to listen? They don't want to miss what is being said. So for the aspects you really want to impress on your customers, you lower your voice. Don't ever raise it. A raised voice means anger, which leads to stress and aggravation. Customers will either take fright, or think you are trying to pressurise them. Nor should you seem to be taking pains to enunciate clearly, for that is also a sign of anger – either that, or condescension, which won't win you any friends. (This can be a problem if you are trying to hide a strong regional accent by speaking carefully.)

Whatever you have to say, if your manner of saying it is a turn-off, people won't listen. And for heaven's sake, be careful what you do say. I have a terrible tendency to make puns. It isn't intentional, my brain does it well enough without any help from me, but it gets me into dreadful trouble at times. I even listened to myself recently telling a newly widowed lady that arranging her husband's affairs would be dead easy! Moral – ensure brain is in gear before releasing clutch on mouth.

Here's another useful reminder for you – a closed mouth gathers no foot. You must, at some time, have found yourself gabbling on, saying things you had no intention of saying, desperately trying to fill an awful silence that has fallen. When two or more people are talking, silence becomes one of those vacuums that Nature is supposed to abhor.

Use it to your advantage. Ask your prospect a question, then shut up. If he doesn't answer immediately, stay shut up. Don't rush in to fill the silence yourself. Shut up and wait him out, smiling politely with your head on one side to show how interested you are in what he's going to tell you. If what he says is just a few words, shut up and wait politely again. Don't let him off the hook, and he will tell you a lot more than he intended to, in the way he says it if not in the words themselves.

Especially in the early stages of getting to know a person (and if you don't get to know them, how will you know which way to angle your pitch?) you want to get a handle on their character. If all they do is answer specific questions, all you will learn is bald facts. What you want is their view of those facts, which gives you an insight into their view of themselves. In office situations, men in particular adopt their business persona, but the more they are encouraged to talk about themselves, the more chance you will get to see behind the 'mask'.

So your questions must be non-directive. As you will see in a minute, you need to listen carefully to the specific words used in the answers. If you ask a leading question, you will get the answer you asked for, not the answer you want. Ask, 'What colour is your lounge?' and you will get a brief answer. Ask, 'What does your lounge look like?' and you will still not get what you need. But ask, 'Tell me about your lounge,' and you will learn not only about the lounge, but a lot more about your prospect.

Non-directive questions are the ones that start with What, When, Where, Who, Why and, best of all, How. The simple question, 'How did you get into this business?' will encourage anyone to talk for ages and, what's more to the point, end up with the conviction that you are a brilliant conversationalist and a charming person. It is also useful when you get one of those awful pauses and can't think of anything else to say.

The other similar question is, 'What do *you* think?', which is especially useful if someone has asked you an embarrassing question like, 'What do you think of the new Tory government?' I guarantee that if you say you think they are dreadful, he'll tell you coldly that he is the chairman of the local Conservative Association, and if you say they're wonderful he'll tell you he stood for Labour and lost. But reply by asking what *he* thinks and he'll tell you exactly where he stands. If you are on the other side of the fence, what do you do? You got it in one – you shut up!

You don't, however, really want to know what his politics are, although it might come in useful. What you should be listening for are the clues that tell you about his favoured method of perception. You are probably already aware that people are either readers or listeners. Some will read a book like this to gain new information and like the outside world to communicate with them in writing. You see them holding a telephone, their attention wandering to the papers on the desk while the person on the other end of the telephone talks, then they say, 'Let me have that in a letter,' and put the phone down. Others would rather go to a lecture or seminar than read a book, would rather use the telephone than receive a letter, would rather you stood in front of them and talked than presented them with a report. Whichever they are, they become impatient if you insist on using the non-favoured method.

There are more subtle shadings than just listening or reading. In the modern world, three of our senses predominate – seeing, listening and feeling. All are available as input devices, but each of us tends to favour one over the others. You might think I've covered two of them already, above, but it isn't as simple as that. The people I have described as readers often come in a different category – thinkers.

Before I go into details on how these people process information and how you tell which is which, I'll tell you why you need to know. As always, you are searching for a handle on them, a way of getting your message across in the most acceptable form. All these people tend to use words which are angled towards their favoured method of perception. Listen carefully and you can slot these words into your speech instead of the ones you normally use. And look carefully at your subject and his chosen environment, for there are visible clues as well.

Thinkers like *information* on paper because they want to be able to refer back to it. They value their ability to *apply logic* to every situation, and want to be sure they *have all the facts right*. (They will hate you if they find out you have supplied them with *incorrect data*.) They value *accuracy*, and will often pause to search for *precisely* the right word, often shutting their eyes to close out the world while they search their data banks. You will not get a quick decision from them, for they like to *weigh all the facts* before giving their *considered opinion*. You will endear yourself to them by keeping quiet while they think and by using such words as *logically*, *precisely* (never roughly or approximately), *conceptually*, and by telling them you would *value* their *thoughts* on the matter.

Visualisers also like facts on paper, but they prefer charts and diagrams to text, so they can *get the picture* better. They like things around them to be neat and orderly. At home, their clothes are always hung up in the proper places, their shoes are lined up in regimental rows and everything on their sideboard will be in a precise place. Their offices are the same; everything is neatly arranged, even their desk drawers, so don't annoy them by cluttering up the place. Don't dump your coat on a chair, or take material out of your briefcase and leave it higgledy-piggledy on the desk instead of placing it in neat piles.

When you give visualisers information, they like to compare it with the *pictures* in their memory. When they do this, some tend to look up to one side; others look into the middle distance, and you should take care not to get in their way where they have to *focus* on you. Although they like *colour*, they do not like colours which clash with their chosen *decorations*, so once you knòw you are dealing with a visualiser, take care to wear neutral colours.

Tell them you have a *clear picture* of their needs, but wonder if a different *perspective* might *shed some light* on things. Perhaps what is needed is a new *point of view*, especially if they have *drawn a blank* previously. Ask them to *show* you how it *looks* to them, so you can have an *image* of what they want. And once you know them better, tell them about your holidays and how great the *views* were, or how much you enjoyed sitting back and *watching* the world go by.

At the opposite extreme are listeners. They tend to be calmer, since they don't spend all their time dashing round to 'see what is going on'. Like visualisers, they retire into their head to process information, but in this case by conducting a conversation with themselves. Don't distract them in this process by talking or making other noises. Occupy your time by looking at the mess around them, for they are not concerned with how things look. The only possessions they prize are devices for making music, and there will probably be some evidence of this in their offices as well as their homes, for music is their comfort as well as their joy.

They often put a hand behind their ear and look sideways when they are thinking, as though to look at that trusty organ. They usually breathe in a very even rhythm and frequently have beautifully modulated voices. And of course they use 'auditory' words. Tell them you *hear what they say*, and that it *rings true*. You don't want to *rattle around* the project, but it is *clicking* into place now, you're getting really *tuned in* to what they want. Your job involves being a *sounding board* for customers, and although their idea might create a little *static* when you get back to head office, you will make sure they *listen* to you this time.

The last major category are feelers. They like *sensations*, to *feel* things, and they will probably *handle* you. Don't worry about this – it is no more than a desire to feel the *texture* of your clothes; they will hand you into a chair, or lay a hand on your shoulder when you have settled. They just like to feel things, so they love dancing and physical sports and jacuzzis, and they love to wear sensuous fabrics. They *move* around in their clothes because they like the way it feels and they have 'feelie' toys on their desks which they play with while you talk to them.

They need to *get to grips* with situations, so they can *remove the stumbling blocks* that give them *bad vibes*. Don't leave a *sour taste* by being *insensitive* to their *heavy* problems. Tell them you *sense* their *uneasiness* over your new product, but that you *feel* they would want to *keep abreast* of the latest developments in these *hard* times. You won't *feel comfortable* unless you can *lighten their load*, and you will be *keeping in touch* until they are *feeling* more *relaxed* about the project. You will be making sure they get plenty of *hands-on* experience with the equipment.

You can't always work out which of these types of person you are dealing with, or you may find you are listening to a mixture of types. But you should still be able to find some key expressions which each person uses and be able to work them into what you are saying. At the very least, make a point of registering whether you are hearing jargonised talk and adapt your own speech to show that you are one of them.

Surely this only works on a one-to-one basis, you will be thinking. What do I do when I am dealing with several people? In a family situation, it is likely that husband and wife (and children), if it is a long-term marriage, will be very alike. Even in a new relationship, both people should be of the same persuasion, or what are they doing together? I know opposites are supposed to be attracted, but they've got to be able to talk to each other, and communication will soon break down if they don't use the same words. But if you do find yourself selling to two disparate partners, it is up to you to work out which is the dominant one. Then address most of your remarks to him or her – most, not all, for if you alienate one of them, they'll queer your pitch when you've gone. The same applies in a business situation, where it is much less likely that they will all be the same. But the subordinates will defer to the decision-maker, even if it is not obvious who that is from the introductions or the seating arrangements.

You are probably also wondering how you are meant to remember which person is what, as you go through your routine of visits. You will expect to see most customers more than once – and there is no reason why you should not make notes on this after an appointment. With a little practice you will find that you identify the sort of person you are dealing with automatically. And so you should – your success is dependent on your ability to handle them.

5 Prospecting

Before you can handle people, you have got to line up some people to see. Don't kid yourself that you will never have to prospect. What do you think your employer wants you for? Any ordinary clerk can take orders if the customer comes in with them – that's why shop assistants are so badly paid. The reason you are on a deal that is linked to your production, with a 'sky's the limit' pay-packet if you are good at your job, is because they want you to go out there and bring the customers in.

Yes, I know some companies do have advertising leads – but only some, not all. And as I've said before, leads are rarely given to beginners. Advertising is expensive and many companies consider paying for advertising as well as employing a sales force is like buying a dog and barking yourself.

You can avoid prospecting yourself by paying someone else to do it for you. There are two ways to do this. The first is to sign up with an organisation that specialises in making appointments for sales people. This tends to be expensive, and their contracts can be rather one-sided: once the appointment is made, you have to pay for it whether or not it is cancelled or postponed, and they often want to be paid within seven days.

The other method is to employ an individual to make your appointments, either on your own or sharing with other people in your office. This is quite a popular arrangement with direct sales people, who are in a better position to claim these expenses against tax. Often the prospector doubles as a secretary, helping you with your paperwork.

Expensive as either of these methods are, they may still be cheaper than spending your own valuable selling time making appointments. You are, after all, a specialist, and your time is too valuable to spend on menial tasks. Economists call this concept 'opportunity cost', but it is no more than common sense and an awareness of the value of your own time.

Sit down and work out how much your actual selling time is worth. Say you work a forty-hour week and spend twenty of those hours doing basic office work. The other twenty hours are genuine selling time, spent seeing customers. If you earn £500 a week from those customers, your selling time is worth £25 an hour. So why are you wasting the other half of your time doing work that someone else would do for a fifth of the amount you could be earning? This of course presupposes that you are earning lots and can afford to pay for help. If not, you will have to do it yourself. Whichever method you decide on – door-knocking, telephoning, mailshots etc, there is one basic decision to be made. Do you favour the shotgun or the rifle approach?

The shotgun method is also known as the 'throwing mud' method (if you throw enough mud against a wall, some of it is bound to stick). It does work, in a fashion, but it is rather a waste of ammunition – your time and resources – in terms of the results it brings. Its only real advantage is that it allows you to play that well-known game, 'Look how *busy* I am!'

It is very easy to confuse activity with accomplishment, but sooner or later you will have to realise that your busy-ness isn't bringing in the money it should. It is probably bringing a lot of refusals, as well, for the simple reason that half the people you are targeting never were and never will be in the market for your product. If you want to make it to the top producers' convention, you'll be more likely to do it with the rifle approach. This involves selecting your target and aiming at it carefully.

Let's assume that you are selling encyclopaedias. If you go round a town, knocking on every door, or working your way through the local phone book from A to Z, sooner or later you will find someone who'll buy. But you will have walked a long way or made a lot of phone calls to make that sale. It makes far more sense to work out who is likely to buy an encyclopaedia, and not waste your time on the ones who aren't. So you can weed out the childless, the penniless and the dumbos who don't even read a newspaper, and concentrate on reasonably affluent parents or grandparents.

Drive round town a little. Find out which are the fee-paying schools and which areas the pupils live in. These parents will not take kindly to door-knocking, but you will at least know which streets to look for in the phone book. Ask if the schools take advertisements for their magazine, or if they need a sponsor for a sports event. Keep an eye on the local paper for birth announcements which say 'A sister for Charles', or news items which tell of a new appointment to the management of a local firm. These often mention children.

Whatever your product, the local paper is a good source of potential customers. Read it with a highlighter in your hand, from cover to cover. People moving into the district, people being promoted or retiring, or having a book published, or winning a prize or service award – all these give you an opportunity to write a personal letter beginning 'Congratulations'. Don't neglect the business sections or the job adverts. These often tell you a lot about a company and its growth areas, and often give a contact name in the department concerned. If it is just a box number, write from your home and ask for an application form to find out who they are.

Find out what local information is on public record. Quite apart from the local library (ours has a notice-board of cards from special interest groups), there are such things as planning application registers at local council offices, the electoral roll, or lists of ratepayers.

When you want to go further afield, start at the reference library. It will have copies of *Yellow Pages* for the whole country (as do main post offices), lists of trade magazines, and various trade directories. The latter (Kompass Regional Sales Guides are the best) give lots of useful information, including names and titles of senior management. Do check these, incidentally, in case people have moved since the directory was published.

If you are looking for individuals rather than busines-ses, you can actually buy lists of names and addresses. These can be lists of shareholders of public companies, which also tell you how many shares the person holds and thus gives an indication of their affluence, or you can obtain lists from commercial list-brokers. These lists can be highly 'qualified'. You can specify a particu-lar socio-economic band (A's, B1's and B2's, say) or people who own shares in more than six companies, or people who are known to be interested in certain areas. You can, for instance, obtain a list of people who have paid over £2000 for a lawnmower, which would be useful if you were selling garden furniture or swimming pools.

List-brokers will sell you an actual list, which comes with a contract forbidding you to use it more than once, or for anything other than the specified purpose, or to let anyone else use it. It will include some 'joker' names, so they will know if you do breach the agreement. They prefer, however, to send out a mailshot for you, in which case you never get to see the list and have to include a reply-paid coupon for prospects to contact you. This time, you are allowed to provide some 'jokers' yourself, to be sure that the stuff is actually despatched.

Whichever way you do it, you should insist on being credited for all returned letters, for they are meant to sell you an up-to-date list, not an old inaccurate one. This is not a cheap exercise, for you have to pay for the names as well as the postage and contents. The normal response rate for mailshots is 2 per cent but you won't convert all of those into sales.

Incidentally, if you make a chance sale to a type of customer (particularly a business) which does not come into your chosen target type, don't treat it as a one-off and forget it. You should have learnt quite a lot about that business, which will stand you in good stead with others in the same field. For this reason, if for no other, it is a good idea to make notes on what you have learned about that customer and his field while it is still fresh in your memory.

The more information you have, especially on commercial prospects, the better. You can only get so far with local papers or directory entries. Both consist of information supplied by the prospect, so what you have is effectively a PR handout. For real, in-depth, useful information, you need to dig a little deeper. If there is a potentially big sale involved, it might be worth getting a local enquiry agency to make some discreet investigations. Otherwise, you'll have to find out for yourself.

A common way for men to do this is some lunchtime drinking at whichever pub is frequented by the target's staff, keeping an ear out for any useful information. That isn't quite so easy for a lone female, so if you want to do that you'll need an accomplice. Alternatively, you could follow some female members of staff to wherever they go for lunch, or to have their hair done, and see if you can strike up an acquaintance to the gossiping level. Another useful source of information is a supplier of non-competitive goods, and it is well worth cultivating some of these on a mutual back-scratching basis.

The sort of information you want to know is: Who really makes the decisions? Does the chief buyer really have purchasing power, or is the managing director so paranoid that he insists on making all decisions over £500? (This is by no means uncommon.) Are they happy with their widget-supplier, or are they looking for a new one? Are they having an economy drive that means they might be interested in your low-price widgets? Has there been a recent change of personnel? A new broom is always looking for a chance to make his mark, and your super widget might be just what he needs to do it. If you can't get this sort of handle on your prospect, you'll have to do it the hard way – going in cold.

Where direct sales are concerned, residential door-knocking is virtually a thing of the past, even for sales men. For a lone woman, it is lunacy even to contemplate it. There are too many nutcases about who would think it was their birthday if they found you on their doorstep. Never mind what your boss says, don't do it.

Cold-calling on businesses is another matter, assuming that they are in a respectable business area. You can get round a lot of companies in a short time on an industrial estate or the commercial centre of town. You might be lucky and find someone who needs some widgets now, but you're more likely to get a series of receptionists telling you, 'He's busy now. I'll give him your card and he'll phone you if he wants anything.'

There is a theory that says this is good for you in the early days – character-forming, or some such nonsense: 'Go on out there and see if you can cope with rejections.' Rubbish! Why should you traipse all over the place, setting yourself up to be knocked down like an Aunt Sally, especially when there are other ways of doing it? If you must do it, at least do it on the telephone where it is a damn sight less personal.

The trouble with appearing unannounced on a doorstep, and to a certain extent also on the telephone, is that you can be tempted to do a mini-presentation. That's a waste of time. You must give yourself the chance to do your product justice and that means having your prospect's full attention. You won't get that until you have gained some rapport with him – and that takes time. It's 'rapport or wrap-up and go!'

The purpose of prospecting is not to sell on the spot, but to get an appointment to do the job properly. To do that, you have to get a conversation going. The more your prospect will talk, the more vocal clues you will get to enable you to modify your own comments, as discussed in the previous chapter. He's only going to listen while he's interested, and he's more likely to be interested if your words get through his perception filter. You should keep this call fairly brief anyway; most people don't want a prolonged discussion with a strange voice, and their attention soon wanders.

Many books on selling will tell you to keep a smile on your face when you talk to prospects on the telephone. It's supposed to make you relax, and transmit confidence down the line, but this is not always appropriate. By all means breeze happiness when you first make contact – after all, you will be pleased to be speaking to a possible customer – but after that, adapt your tones to the response you get, or to the needs of your product. If you were an undertaker, would you take kindly to a salesperson who exuded happiness about their new model coffin handles? They might even come along and be happy in your Chapel of Rest, where the bereaved might see them!

Some books on selling also tell you to keep your phone calls confined to a prepared script. I've had several very wooden calls from people obviously reading such a script. It throws them completely when I refuse to play the game and won't give the answers their script tells them I will. That's the snag with such scripts – the prospect doesn't have a copy of it, and tends to ask awkward questions. By all means have a prepared plan, or a list of topics to cover. This keeps you in control of the situation and helps you remember everything you need to say. Otherwise, it is very easy to think you've said something to this person, when actually you said it to the last one. Listen to any salesperson make a sequence of calls, and if they do not tick off a list as they go, I guarantee they'll miss something crucial on half of them.

Do keep a record of your calls, too. All you need is name, address and number, when you called, the response, and any action needed. That way you won't call the same person twice, and you can swap lists with the others in the office to avoid duplication. And for heaven's sake, if you are working your way through a phone directory, mark the number you are calling now. Anyone who gets an agreement for an appointment, then asks for the prospect's name and address, deserves to get the big PO – and probably will!

It is easier when you are following up letters. All you

have to do there is write the phone numbers on the copies and work your way through them, marking the responses as you go. You will probably have to go through your prepared call plan in this case as well, for the purpose of a good pre-approach letter is no more than to warm the cold prospect up a little.

'Hello, I'm your friendly neighbourhood widget expert. We have a lovely range of widgets, and I'd like to meet you and tell you all about them. I'll phone you next week for an appointment.' That's what a pre-approach letter should say. You can't close a sale unless you get in front of the customer, so why do people send out dreadful long-winded sales letters that drone on about the product? They are an instant turn-off, and 99.9 per cent of them go straight in the bin. So do letters with a giveaway company frank or logo on the envelope, and so do letters with bad typing or misspelt names. Would you want to do business with someone who was too lazy to get your name right?

If you want people to read your letters themselves, use plain envelopes, hand-write them and use a proper stamp. It won't do any harm to hand-write the letter as well (if it is to a business, this will get it past the secretary to the desk you want it on). Since you really should keep the message as short as the one above, although it obviously shouldn't be as breathless, it won't hurt you to write it a few times each day. If you must send technical material, send it in the form of brochures and add a PS: 'Brochures enclosed for your perusal.'

The problem with sending brochures, even to businesses, is that you have given the prospect an excuse not to see you. He has all he needs in the brochures, thank you, and he'll call you when he needs something. There is also a type of private individual, often the retired and poorly-off, who likes to collect brochures. They have no intention of buying, but they like to dream and have the postman bring them nice fat envelopes.

What you want is to make appointments, not contributions to someone's brochure collection, nor merely to have a nice chat on the telephone. Sooner or later, you've got to ask the question, but it had better be the right one. Not, 'Can I come and see you then?' but, 'Would three o'clock on Thursday suit you, or shall we make it twelve o'clock on Monday?' It's very difficult to say anything other than 'Yes' to that sort of question, so people will agree to see you, thinking that they'll listen to your pitch and then say No. But you won't let them do that so easily, will you? It takes a real tough cookie to be nasty to a woman face to face, but it's very easy on the telephone. Word the fatal question wrongly and you'll get the wrong answer – the dreaded *rejection*.

This is the thing that stops most sales careers dead in their tracks before they've even got properly started. There's even a psychological term for it – 'rejection pressure'. Like many things, the label has taken on a life of its own, far greater than the problem itself, and the simple fear that someone might say No has become a great bogeyman.

When you say to your milkman, 'No, I don't want any cream this week,' he doesn't go off contemplating suicide because you've rejected him. All he concludes from the exchange is that you don't want any cream. So why should you get in a tizz when someone says, 'No, I don't want any widgets,' or even, 'Go away, I don't want your bloody widgets!' What this person means is that he does not want widgets, perhaps even that he is getting a little tired of people trying to sell him widgets when he doesn't want them. What he does not mean is that you,

Eloisa Bloggs, representative of The International Widget Group Ltd, are a dreadful person, a blot on the landscape, a disgrace to humanity and that you don't deserve to live. So why should you assume that that is what he means? Why choose to decide you have been rejected, when you should be choosing to decide that this town is full of stupid people who wouldn't know a good widget if they had one given to them for Christmas? Take yourself off somewhere where they have the good sense to appreciate you and your beautiful widgets. Just don't let the prospect know you think he is a crass idiot for not buying your widgets. Smile politely and thank him for his time, and he will remember you another day when he does want a widget.

By the way, I am assuming that these people who are giving you answers which you have chosen to label rejection are all strangers. So why are you trying to do business with strangers? Haven't you got any friends? Everyone, no matter who they are, would rather do business with a friend than a stranger. So make friends!

The obvious people to make friends with are people you have already sold to. It is the easiest thing in the world to do, and yet so few people bother to do it. All you need to do is make sure that your customers are happy with the product – then they'll be happy with you. If there's one good way to alienate a customer, it is to take the order and never go near him again, so keep in touch. Send cards at Christmas and birthdays or other anniversaries, keeping your ears pinned back for news about them so you can telephone and say, 'Hi – I just heard the news.' If you offer to do anything for them, *do it*. There are so many people who break promises, that a reputation for keeping them will put you high up in everyone's estimation.

A customer who holds you in esteem is a customer who will recommend you to his friends and acquaintances. He will not object if you go to him and ask for some referrals. You can be quite open about it. 'I need some more business and I wondered who you might know that I can go and see.' If he likes you, he will be happy to help, but this is one of those rare times when you need to ask the direct question, 'Who do you know that might buy some widgets?' If necessary, break it down further, '– in your road, golf club, at work, etc.?' 'Who do you know?' on its own is a very wide question, but if you qualify it you will blinker your prospect's thinking and send him down the routes that bring results.

You have other friends who may one day become customers. If you want to succeed in selling without too much effort, you should consciously take the trouble to make friends of people who are, or will be, influential. Don't just think of today's sale, cultivate people who will secure your future success. If you can do someone a business favour, do so and consider it an investment in your future. Such gestures are remembered, without your needing to do anything as crude as indicating, 'You owe me one.'

A good place to make useful friends is the business conference or seminar. You aren't naive enough to think that people really go to listen to the speeches, are you? Conferences are for brain-picking, for staying sober while drunken rival delegates spill the beans on their company's plans, and for making useful contacts. If your company has a stand at an exhibition, by all means go, but be sure that you have the freedom to roam about. (Wear your usual business clothes. If they want dolly birds on the stand, let them hire them from an agency – you are not a sex object.)

Travel first-class like other business people do, and take any available chance to introduce yourself and hand over a card. You should get one back in return, and you've got another contact. Go to business parties, political parties, Chamber of Commerce functions and private parties given by business people. With the latter, keep a low profile. It is not good manners to muscle in on someone else's game, and you won't be asked again if you do.

Take the trouble to cultivate influential people. Every small town, and a lot of big ones, has the legendary cartel of solicitors, accountants, estate agents and bank managers. If you can get into that sort of circle, your future is assured. Buy these influencers lunch. They are fully aware that there is no such thing as a free lunch and they won't be dim enough to think that it's their body you're after. At least, they shouldn't, or you should be bright enough to fend them off gently. We don't want to get a reputation as the town bicycle, do we? So lay off the booze at lunch – it loosens the tongue, not to mention the inhibitions, and there are still plenty of people around who think it isn't ladylike. These days, plenty of people drink mineral water and you can always plead an appointment in the afternoon.

To avoid any difficulties at bill-paying time, it is a good idea to arrive a little early and warn the *maître d'* that you want the bill. Better still, pop out to the loo at coffee-time and pay it then. That way, there won't be any difficulties later. No waiter giving it to the man, no chauvinistic sensibilities inflamed – and no neat shifting of obligations, either!

6 Presentation techniques

So there you are, actually in front of a prospect. You're dressed right, you've sussed him out and got the rapport going. Now what?

Now you are going to make a presentation, that's what. Before you fling this book across the room, muttering, 'Stupid woman, of course I'm going to make a presentation! That's what I'm there for!' just bear with me a little longer. Let's put it another way – you are going to present your product to the prospect. Then you will answer queries, field objections and, hopefully, make a sale.

What you should not be doing, at any point, is begging your prospect to buy. Unfortunately, far too many women do just that without realising it. They say, 'Would you mind if . . .?' and don't realise that this constitutes an apology, or they make statements which end in a rising inflection that turns them into questions, or they add one of those dreadful ingratiating Snoopy smiles as though they hope for a pat on the head.

Questions are for learning things, and smiles are to show pleasure and confidence. Neither should be used to apologise for your presence – there is no need to do that at all. The trouble is that despite all the shouting about liberation and equality, many of us have been conditioned by our upbringing or marriages to be submissive. We have learnt to defer to other people's wishes rather than to pursue our own.

Never forget that, with rare exceptions, a sales interview is an intrusion. You have persuaded the prospect that he ought to see you, but on the whole his wish is probably that you should go away and leave him in peace. This is, however, no time for you to be a good girl and defer to his wishes.

People who defer are subordinate. Most businessmen prefer to do business with their equals, and some actually feel insulted if they think they are not doing so. They also prefer to do business with winners, so if you come across a prickly man who tries any of the standard male domination ploys, it might be worth a little side-track to give him some subtle propaganda about how successful you are. It's easy enough to do. Praise the product, say how well it is selling, then slip in a little comment about how high you are up the sales league. Never mind the fine detail on this one – tell him you were number six last month, and press on with the presentation before you have to explain that there are only six of you in your branch, which happened to be bottom branch!

Practise the postures of authority and the cool confident speech of authority. Remember that people with high status don't move around a lot (they just stay still and wait for subordinates to fetch and carry), so keep your gestures and body movement under control. Be careful not to go to the other extreme and strike a pose – this will require attention to maintain, and you need all your attention on what you are saying and how it is being received.

One of the main reasons the 'canned pitch' doesn't work is that it presupposes that every prospect is the same. They aren't, and until you learn to read the feedback and amend your presentation accordingly, you won't get very far. This means that you must have all the facts in your head, where you can juggle them and pull out whatever is needed.

Let's suppose you are selling a car to a man who looks about forty-five. He hasn't said who it is for and you missed an earlier opportunity to ask. He's just asked about performance, so you quote the car's top speed. He gives a little frown. This is your cue to pause and ask who is going to be driving it. He says it is for his son, so that little frown should tell you he's worried about the boy's driving. You would be foolish to bang on about power and acceleration. Drop that line and go straight into your safety routine, emphasising the excellent brakes, skid-resistant tyres and so on.

There are umpteen reasons for buying. The father above could be buying his son a car as a gesture of love, for his own convenience (fed up with having to drive the boy around), self-preservation (the boy keeps borrowing his car) or vanity (doesn't want the neighbours to see the boy waiting for buses and think he can't afford a car); but the main factor which will influence his decision on *which* car he buys is the avoidance of worry. In another domestic situation it might be pride of ownership or a desire for self-improvement. In a business situation, you may be naive enough to think the main motive is that your product will help to increase profits, but this is not always so. Prestige and status considerations are just as important – for instance, very few big cars are bought new by private individuals. They mostly go to companies, who give them to their senior executives.

Your task is to discover the dominant motive and angle your pitch towards it. Never mind that it isn't the reason most people buy the product, or even the reason you would buy the product. If the prospect seems to think it is a good enough reason to spend his money, that's all you need to know.

It's an old selling adage that you sell 'the sizzle, not the sausage' or 'the benefit rather than the product'. Nevertheless, with all but the experienced cynical professional buyer, what you are really selling is a dream. 'Buy our double glazing and your draughty house will become a cosy home.' 'Buy our fitted bathroom and you can lie back in bubbles like a film star.' 'Buy our loan and go on an exotic holiday.' 'Buy our widgets and the customers will flood into your shop and make your fortune.' 'Buy our widget-maker and drive your competitors out of business.'

OK, so you're really a dream merchant. But don't you also have a dream? The one about all the prospects who say Yes, the one where you go back to the office and put a sheaf of orders on your boss's desk, where he takes your name tag and moves it to the top of the league board, where you get your photograph in the company magazine and get first prize at the annual convention? QED – help your customers realise their dreams and they will help with yours.

Not only must your presentation be angled towards realising the customer's intimated or stated desire, so must your props. You should know your brochures, and have them organised, well enough to be able to produce the right one to back up what you've been saying. Or rather, you should be able to lay hands immediately on the one you want, which is not quite the same thing. I know one brilliant lady who has a routine that involves selecting a brochure, looking at it, frowning, then putting it back and handing over a different one. They always ask, 'What was the other one?' 'Oh, that,' she says, 'that's the de luxe range. You won't be able to afford that.' She only uses this routine when she judges that keeping up appearances is important, but tells me it never fails.

Your brochures must always be immaculate – no tired

corners or grubby fronts. Get into the habit of checking and replenishing your stock at least once a week, and ditching all your copies of anything that has been superseded. If you feel that there is a gap in the range of handouts, and you've been with the company a while, there is no reason why you should not ask for some new designs. Most companies are only too pleased to get suggestions from the people at the sharp end, as long as they aren't too expensive to implement.

If you carry samples, or a demonstration kit or machine, these too must be immaculate. Treat them as if you love them. If you're telling the customer that the product is wonderful, how can you justify abusing it? Make sure that demonstration machines work properly and that you know exactly how to make them perform. There is no quicker way to blow a sale than to fumble with a recalcitrant machine.

Keep machines and samples and visual aids out of the way until you are ready to use them, then you can indulge in a little showmanship by producing them with a 'Tah-rah!' If they are in sight from the beginning, they distract attention from what you are saying. If you are daft enough to put them where the customer can get his hands on them, he will inevitably play with them and miss the whole of your pitch. Sod's law also says that the product will probably attack him!

If you are making your presentation to a group of people rather than an individual, they will not only play with the product, but will also discuss it instead of paying attention to you. It's no good your spreading the chairs out in the hope of preventing this – they'll just lean over or talk louder.

Presenting to a group is a whole new game. If you've never done any public speaking you would be wise to go on a course to get some practice in dealing with an audience. On a one-to-one basis you can usually get away with forgetting your lines, and if you sense that things are going badly you can wind it up and get out fairly easily. You can't pack up in the middle of a presentation to a group; nor can you run away from them if you want to retain your credibility in your chosen industry. It is impossible to have eye contact with the whole group at once, which means that you have to keep looking at different people, or at the wall behind them, so they'll wonder why you have shifty eyes or won't look at them.

When it comes to question time, be prepared for a long session. They'll spark each other off, and if they are all from the same company, they'll have their hierarchical relationships to play with as well. Apart from those who want to impress their superiors or peers with their grasp of the subject, there is often a know-it-all who just likes the sound of his own voice. You can't avoid this, but you can lessen the problem by addressing your presentation to the senior person there and asking him (by name if possible) if he has any questions. It is then up to him to suggest that the others may have some, but since the invitation has come from him, they are less likely to play clever-clever with you.

How do you know who he is, if you haven't been introduced and there are no name tags? Easy – by the place he picks to sit, by the way he enters the room, and by the deference with which he is treated. He will always sit at the 'head' of the table, in which case you should try to sit opposite (never next to him, for this means you will have your back to the others when you address him, or to him when you address the others). In a bigger room or hall, where there are rows of seats, he will be in the centre of the front row, next to the aisle if there is one. This position allows him to come in last (or leave early) and see all his minions before he sits. In any situation where you are in the room before the group arrives, he will usually lead the way through the door. If you have control over the seating, make sure he has his back to a wall.

If he does arrive attended by a crowd of acolytes, you will get a fair idea of his ego by observing the way they behave. If they are respectful but easy with him, he is probably reasonable and well-adjusted. But if they watch him all the time and wait to follow his lead before reacting, you may be dealing with a monster ego. Be prepared to go along with it if you really want the business.

When you are part of a team giving major presentations to the public or a mixed bag of business people, you'll need to attend the rehearsals and de-briefs. If the team does not already hold these, see if you can persuade them, for you do not need the embarrassment of being part of a sloppy performance. There should actually be a full 'dress' rehearsal, with each person going through their whole routine of speaking, handling the props and audio-visual aids, all the way down to writing on the flip-charts.

The members of the team who are not 'on stage' should situate themselves about the room to check how each speaker sounds and looks, and whether the flip-charts or screens can be seen from every position. I've been to many presentations where the lighting or acoustics have been so patchy that it was obvious that no one thought to check them. Even the minor point of where the easel is situated needs careful attention if everyone is to be able to see it.

Can you actually write legibly on a flip-chart or blackboard? Have you practised? Don't you think you should? And isn't it time someone thought of something better than moving a blank piece of paper down the overhead projector slide to reveal one line at a time? I've never seen anyone who doesn't make a pig's breakfast of it.

Even the part of the room you stand in can be important, especially on a sunny day and if you are wearing something flimsy. If you do not go through your routine, your colleagues will not be able to warn you that they can see through your skirt at a certain spot, or that you have rubbed all the powder off your nose, or that you have a distracting habit of scratching your ear, or that your hand shakes when you are nervous – which makes your papers rustle loud enough to drown out half of what you are saying. (Get a clipboard!)

And what, exactly, are you saying? Who wrote the words? The trouble with standing up in public and reading (or reciting) someone else's words is that they may not conform to your own speech patterns and you will stumble over them. Even if you are word perfect (you'd better be) it will still sound stilted and as though you don't know your subject. Mind you, it can sound that way even when you write your own script if you put in words you don't usually use. Far better to have headline cards and speak off the cuff.

Watch out for abbreviations, too. They can come over very badly if they are awkward letters. I remember listening to one speaker on investments who kept referring to 'P/E ratios'. I suspect that someone had told him to say it carefully, because every time he gave a noticeable pause and said, 'Peeyah – Eeyah – ratios.' It would have been much easier to say the whole thing – 'Price/Earnings ratios'.

Someone should be timing the event, and its component parts, with a stop-watch. Then you can decide if the weighting is right, or if the longer items should be moved or cut. Keep these timings, for part of the de-brief must be whether anyone has noticed any signs of restlessness in the audience, or wandering attention.

You will of course get slightly different reactions from different audiences, but do talk those reactions over and make changes if you think they are necessary. Never forget that you are dealing with just that – an audience. In today's world, people are accustomed to the super-sophisticated presentations they see on television, and they will soon decide that you aren't much good at your job if you don't match up to that sort of professionalism.

As a woman, you may need to walk a delicate tightrope between making sure that the meeting and greeting aspect is done properly, and getting lumbered with the female 'support' role of organising things yourself. Let me tell you about one badly managed presentation I attended last year and you'll see what I mean. It was held at our local Chamber of Commerce building, in their main hall, which they had rented to the organisers. Although it was not their 'do', their reception staff could have been a lot more helpful. The invitation said 'six-thirty for seven o'clock' and 'Buffet', so I assumed that the buffet would follow the presentation, had a reasonably large lunch to carry me through the evening and told my fiancé that I would be eating out and latish home. I stayed at work until six-fifteen, then strolled the mile to the edge of the business section of town.

The organisers did not appear until seven-fifteen, but the signs led to the bar where the steward expected me to pay for my drink, after demanding whether I was a member. I was not amused, nor did I particularly enjoy trying to make polite conversation with the only other female there. All the men seemed to know each other and I was not anxious to join their golf conversation.

I was just about to give up and go home when the presentation team arrived, rolled back the partition to the hall and removed a cloth that was shrouding some rather dry sandwiches. 'Do have something to eat,' they said expansively, and retired into a corner to unpack their boxes. It was gone eight o'clock before they got started on the presentation. The introduction was slick enough, but it was followed by the company's founder who spent ten minutes telling us about all the problems they'd had with the product in its early days. To be fair, once he'd got past that bit, he was very interesting and really knew his stuff, but the next speaker was hesitant and got into a real mess with the overhead projector.

It finally ended at ten, by which time it was dark. No one had thought of organising taxis, and I was not about to walk through dark streets to a bus stop on the wrong side of town. It took some argument before they found me a telephone in a dingy stockroom and I was able to phone for my fiancé to fetch me. Fortunately I only lived a couple of miles away, but I was not at all pleased with the evening. No sale!

Annoying prospects with this sort of mismanagement is a stupid way to throw away a sale. Boring them with dull presentations is another, and so is persisting with attempts to 'close' when they've made it clear that they are not ready to buy just yet. I was ready to buy a new word-processor last year, planning to purchase when an investment bond matured. I started looking at various models good and early, and soon decided which one I wanted. I made it quite clear that the money wasn't available for several months, but the salesman rang me every week to ask if I'd made up my mind yet. I'm still using the old machine!

Most books on selling give at least a dozen reasons why a prospect does not buy. There are really only three — he doesn't want it, he can't afford it or he doesn't like you. There is nothing you can do about any of these, although you will learn with experience whether the first two statements are genuine or a preliminary to haggling over the price.

Most of what are usually labelled 'objections' are actually pleas for reassurance that they are doing the right thing. The longer you can put off answering them, the less of a problem they become, and if you keep your cool you can turn 'What about . . . ?' into obtaining more information on the prospect. 'Does that present a problem?' you ask, and they will then tell you in great detail why it might be a problem. It's up to you to reassure them on all the points, and add a few more plus points on aspects they have revealed as being important to them. You do not, in this process, have to tell them of all the warts on the product, unless they really do impinge on the problem area. If that is the case, it would be unethical to keep quiet, and although to do so might win you a sale, it won't win you any friends.

Learn to tell the difference between genuine questions for information, and questions used as a dominance ploy. Many women will actually stop in their tracks and answer a direct question, as if there were no option. The option, which always exists, is to say firmly, 'I'll be getting to that later,' and carry on.

Once the customer is asking genuine questions about the product, he is usually ready to buy. The only snag is that while he may have made up his mind that he wants a widget, he may not be sure whose widget he wants. The commonest question is, 'How does it compare with the Bloggs Alpha De Luxe Widget?' This is not your cue to badmouth the competition. That's petty, and people don't like it. It's far better to play up your widget's good points, and better yet to turn the question back on them by asking which aspects they really care about.

Look for areas where you can agree with each other. Don't argue or try to tell him he's wrong, or he'll want to defend himself on that particular issue and soon convince himself that it presents an insurmountable problem. If you can reach agreement on little things, you can probably do it on the big issues. 'Yes, it is rather a bright blue. Yes, it does look rather small. Mind you, it is deceptive. Look in here – can you see how far the boot goes under the back seats?'

'Yes,' he says, and now he's agreeing with you.

Keep it up and he'll soon say Yes to the big question: 'Then we're agreed that this one is suitable and we'll go ahead, shall we?' And you know what you do when you've asked that question, don't you? That's right, you shut up and wait for him to make his decision. If he asks a question, keep your answer as short as you can, and let him get back to his deciding without the distraction of your voice. You can't influence him at this stage, and you don't want to distract him or give him an excuse to 'go away and think it over'. Just wait him out, and sooner or later he'll say Yes or No.

This is called closing, and is another area of selling that has had whole tomes devoted to it. There are even people who make a living lecturing on it. I can't imagine why. It's as simple as this – tell the customer everything he wants to know, pick your time and ask him if he's ready to buy. Yet you'd be amazed how many salespeople go through their whole routine with a prospect and never get around to asking that basic question: 'Do you want it?'

Incidentally, don't be frightened to use the word 'sign'. If you need a signature, say so; don't beat about the bush with euphemisms like 'OK it'. People know they have to sign when they buy things, so you might as well come out with it.

You don't always get to that stage in one interview, although with most consumer goods or services you should make it by the second. But that is a fairly simple situation, where the prices are fixed (more or less) and the only variations on these are colour or finish. In a commercial situation it is far more complicated. You may need to go through a long sequence of specifications and drawings before you can consider anything as simple as price – not that that is simple, either. There are so many variables when you are negotiating a substantial contract that you need to know far more than what the product costs. You need to know what it costs to produce, finish, package, pack, insure and deliver. And you need to know how much your company's bank loans are costing. When you've got all that lot in your head, you can start juggling and haggling until you and the customer can reach a mutually satisfactory solution.

You might be able to shift some of the production costs if the customer will accept the product unpainted, or supply his own inspectors at your factory, or take it in boxes of five hundred instead of fifty. If he wants it in a hurry, you may have to pay overtime rates to get it done in time, but then perhaps he only needs the first batch in a hurry and will take the rest over a longer period. Maybe he'll fetch it instead of your having to deliver, or maybe he'll arrange (and pay for) the transport insurance. Maybe he is so anxious to be the only one to retail it that he'll pay a premium for an exclusive dealership, or does he think that means you should chip in with some of his advertising costs? Does he think big quantities mean longer credit, or will he pay early to earn a discount?

If all that doesn't offer enough options, the export situation is even more fun. Barter is fashionable again, so you not only have to sell your product, you also have to sell the product you get in return. You sell them tractors, they pay you in coffee. Or they send the coffee to Hassan in Bahrain and he pays you in pearls.

There's no way you're going to agree on that lot in one session. You'll be back several times, finalising one bit at a time, calling in various experts at different stages, and checking back with your boss all the way. Never mind – it'll be a big deal, and big deals carry big commission.

7 Selling to women

I have been writing as though every prospect you encounter will be a man or a married couple, but of course they won't. In a business situation, more and more women are rising to the managerial levels where they will be making purchasing decisions. Outside businesses, these women managers and many other working women are earning high enough salaries to constitute a large consumer sector. In their homes, many more women these days hold the family cheque-book and make the decisions about major purchases.

They are all sick and tired of being patronised by stupid salesmen who talk down to them. It must have happened to you – the imbecile at the garage who thought your only interest in the car was its colour and where to put your handbag; the fool at the hi-fi shop who suggested you should bring your husband to 'help you decide' which CD-player to buy; the creep at the mortgage brokers who thought you hadn't the wit to know the difference between endowment or repayment mortgages; and all the others.

There is a vast, still almost untapped, market out there of women who are fed up with trying to buy from stupid men. Part of the problem is that many salesmen come from working-class backgrounds, where the only money women handle is the folding stuff their men hand over on Friday night. These men are not used to independent women, and the idea that women might earn as much, or more, than they do makes them feel very uneasy. They resort to treating you as they would their mum, sister or daughter, and they have no concept of how much it offends. This doesn't happen in places that supply what used to be called 'the carriage trade'. Go upmarket and you will find the treatment very different. There, salespeople are used to women having their own money and wouldn't dream of patronising them.

It probably hasn't occurred to you that you might be in danger of doing just that to female prospects, but it is a very real danger, particularly if you spend most of your time in male company. The attitudinal traits of our constant companions are insidiously catching, especially if you are striving to be accepted by these companions. The behaviour that is appropriate in exclusively male company is not always appropriate when you are dealing with females, and the male trait of patronising women is totally inappropriate at any time.

There is another trap to beware when you are dealing with a housewife. If you are an independent working girl, it is easy to assume that a woman who does not have a job, nor young children to account for her stay-at-home life-style, is either thick or a cop-out. Neither is necessarily true. There is a revolution brewing against the tyranny of 'liberation', and the pendulum is swinging back the other way. Many intelligent women are now electing to stay at home permanently – but how do you know that your prospect doesn't work at home with a computer link, or isn't studying for a doctorate?

The moral here is that you should not make any assumptions before meeting, or jump to any conclusions on first observations when you do meet; you should certainly not decide how to treat the lady until you have met her. The approach that will get you into most trouble is, 'We're all girls together.' That one even annoys other women in the same line of work as you, let alone those who aren't.

Go back to basics. The only thing you know for sure about this person is that she is the same gender as you. You may have a few more basic facts about her, but unless you have had a detailed discussion about her with another woman who has sold to her, you are going to have to do it the hard way, just like you would with a man.

You can't even assume that she will respond well to a woman selling. Yes, lots of women would, but there are also a lot of women who wouldn't, who would actually feel cheated if they weren't confronted by a man. It would spoil all the comfortable games they play to pad out their lives and shift the blame for their problems. There's 'I'm only a defenceless little woman' ('but let anything go wrong with the product and watch me scream "Rape!" '), or 'I may be a dumb broad' ('but I've got long eyelashes and maybe you'll throw in some freebies if I flutter them at you suggestively') – both of which need a man to play at all – and several others like 'I'll have to ask my husband' ('I wish I hadn't started this – I don't want it, but I haven't got the guts to say so'), which theoretically could be played with a woman, but rarely is because they know it wouldn't work.

Then there are various types who are just good old-fashioned jealous of your freedom. They may run their life like a game of 'Wooden leg' ('I could have been an Olympic runner if I didn't have a wooden leg' or, in this case, 'I can't do anything as nasty as go out and earn a living, I'm a woman!'), and along you come and ruin the whole thing. They may just be beastly to you straight out, or they may disguise it with cries of, 'What's a nice girl like you . . . ? (doing with a nasty job like selling)', which really means, 'You can't possibly be a nice girl.'

These are the women who will think you are after their husband. The only way you will have a chance of staying in their house long enough to make a sale is to be totally businesslike with both of them. Keep your attention on her and aim your presentation at her. Don't let your eyes wander round the room, certainly not in his direction unless he speaks to you, and even then keep your eye contact to a minimum. If you have an opportunity to make a remark about your own husband/fiancé/boy-friend do so (a nice remark, not a bitchy one). If you have to go back to the house for a repeat visit, it might even be worth thinking of wearing something masculine or demure.

The same sort of lady can even manage to be jealous if you are there to sell to her son. Let's face it, if he is old enough to have money to buy from you, he'd be living away from home if he wasn't under her thumb. The best way to deal with this is to try and make her your ally, in his interest, not against him. It's a very tricky situation if she doesn't want him to have your product. Any sign that you are siding with her and he'll think you are ganging up on him; any sign that you are siding with him against her and she'll get to work on him after you've gone. Far better to cut the interview short and think of a reason why he ought to come and see you in your office.

There is one other sort of jealous lady who needs to be handled carefully – the secretary. It is part of a sec-retary's job to protect her boss from the outside world, and some produce a very passable imitation of a tigress with cubs. Some will even reject the status and comfort of their own office in favour of a desk outside the boss's, if that gives a better line of sight to the main door and approaching predators.

Don't do anything to antagonise her or, like the fond

mama, she'll dump the deal after you've gone. She may bitterly resent her paltry salary without having the nerve to take a job like yours. She will have a stack of rationalisations on why she shouldn't take the plunge, but they won't stop her hating you for doing what she daren't. Keep in her good books by talking to her as respectfully as you will her boss, and let her imagine that you are asking her permission to pass the hallowed portals. And if you are selling any form of office equipment or supplies, do not forget that, while her boss may sign the order forms, she is the one who will be using the stuff and she can easily influence the decision.

Of course you mustn't make the stupid, classic mistake of assuming that all females in offices must be secretaries. It is not just visiting men who do it, women do it too. It seems to be an extension of, 'I'm the greatest (brilliant saleswoman, etc.)' to arrive at, 'I'm unique, there can't be any other women doing jobs as high-powered as mine.' This attitude gets up men's noses as well as women's, so knock it off. And don't forget that the average woman manager takes a perverse pleasure in going along with your assumption until you have dug a really big hole for her to push you into with her casual revelation that she *is* the boss. Nor is it tactful to make any reference to the fact that she is a female in a senior position, especially if it is a rarity in that particular industry. That may awaken her lurking fears of being there as a token and she won't thank you for it. Personal remarks are for personal friends and, in a business situation, if you wouldn't say it to a man, you shouldn't say it to a woman.

Don't comment on her office, her clothes or her hair. If you know her fairly well, it is in order to remark on how well she looks, but then you could say that to a man as well. About the only thing you should do that is different from the way you would treat a man is to check her ring finger and ask whether she likes to be addressed as Mrs, Miss or Ms. Married women may use their maiden name at work (and outside) and preferences vary on the use of Ms.

If you have any sales 'tricks' in your repertoire, think twice before using them with a woman. She will spot them for what they are straight away. Remember 'quadrophonic' sound, and the 'two separate speakers for each ear'? All the women I mentioned it to immediately said it was silly because you only have one ear on each side, but there were plenty of men running round enthusing about how wonderful they were!

Many men only listen to the *sound* of what you say rather than the content. They are waiting for you to stop talking so they can have their turn. The more you have to say about the product, the better they assume it must be. But women are not usually in such a hurry to talk that we don't listen to the *content* of the speech.

It should be easy enough to see whether she is following you word for word by her reactions as you speak. This is equally valid when you are dealing with men, but they tend to put their poker faces on for sales presentations and the changes you will be looking for are less easy to spot than with a woman.

Part of your early rapport-establishing work should include some simple Yes or No questions: 'Have you been on holiday yet?', 'Do you drive in to work?' Most people respond with more than a verbal answer, and the response is slightly different for agreement than disagreement. They will move their head slightly one way or the other, change their breathing rate, even change skin colour slightly. By the time the interview has got to the point where you launch into your long sales spiel, you should know which signs to watch for in this person. 'Yes' signs, and you pursue the track you are on; 'No' signs, and it's time for a change; a series of 'No' signs, and you'd better get back to a point where you can gain agreement and keep gaining it.

The essence of selling is communication. If you can't communicate your product's excellence, you're not going to sell a lot. Good communicating is not just a question of talking at a prospect – you need to remain constantly alert for feedback and for the need to vary your approach. If you find this difficult, and prospects keep fading out on you, or if you start getting hostile responses, it is time for some ruthless self-analysis. Then ask your boss for some practice with a colleague and, if possible, a video-tape. Assuming that you are already technically competent, you need to learn to think on your feet.

One area that might create hostility in a woman is the manner in which you ask questions. I've already mentioned the male habit of throwing questions at you, demanding that you stop what you are doing immediately to answer them. It is very annoying, even if you refuse to play, and if you happen to do it to a woman who has had it done to her by a man, she'll remember and hate you. Like all memories, anything that triggers an incident in your memory produces the whole set of reactions connected with the incident. It must have happened to you – a scent or a piece of music that brings back a long-forgotten incident in its entirety. This is why lovers make such a fuss about 'our song' – every time they hear it, it brings back all the first raptures of new-found love.

You can use these triggers positively. Hypnotists use

them a lot, sometimes calling them 'anchors' instead of triggers. If your prospect has given you an indication that you have hit on one – for instance, your 'Have you been on holiday yet?' question may have produced a fond smile and, 'Oh yes, we went back to Sorrento, where we had our honeymoon' – you know that a mention of holidays or honeymoons should trigger a happy memory that makes your prospect feel good.

Pull the wrong trigger, however, and you will make her feel bad. We've all had the abrupt 'Tell me, now!' experience, so be careful how you ask for crucial information. One very gentle and flattering way to gain this information is to word your question as a statement. 'I've been wondering why . . .' implies that you are very interested in this lady and want to know more about her.

There is another 'reversion' technique which is very useful, this time not to obtain information, but to put a thought firmly into your prospect's head. It's known as a 'negative command'. If I tell you not to think about yellow elephants, you have no choice but to think about them. You have to, to make sense of what I said.

If I am trying to sell a life assurance policy to your husband, and you and he both think it costs too much, nothing I say about benefits and bonuses will help. That will only make you more convinced that you'd rather have jam today than at some nebulous time in the future. Even if I state that it will keep the family secure if he dies, you won't accept that. Death is all too easy to shut out of your mind. But if I say, 'I don't want you to lie awake at night thinking about how horrid it would be to be a poor widow,' you'll be on the phone to me in the morning asking when he can sign the forms.

Whatever the situation, and whatever your product, you ought to be able to think of something on these lines.

One major advantage about selling to women is that we do have a wealth of experience in common. You and your prospect may be at opposite ends of the spectrum socially, religiously or ethnically, but you are both likely to have the same feelings for your menfolk and your children, the same domestic duties and problems and, if she also works, the same range of problems with men at work.

This does not mean that you should let yourself get deeply involved in her problems, whether at home or at work. With the latter, she would do better to join a women's network, and so would you. These groups help in the best possible way – they make you realise that your problems are not unique, and they give you access to ways in which other women have tackled the situations you now face. Networks are also, incidentally, a good source of prospects.

With domestic problems, your best bet is also to pass on useful names. By all means make mildly sympathetic noises if your prospect wants to confide in you, but remember that you are there to sell, not act as a social worker or marriage guidance counsellor. These are both jobs which call for special training, not well-meaning advice of the 'If I were you ...' variety.

In fact, if it turns out that the woman is in the middle of major emotional difficulties, you would do best to withdraw as tactfully as you can. You should be devoting all your energies to running your own life, not wasting them by getting involved in what frequently turn out to be other people's self-inflicted traumas. It is not unknown for such women to make suicidal phone calls to your home in the early hours of the morning, or worse, to your office in the middle of the day.

So keep your distance from your customers until you

are absolutely sure that you want them to become close friends. On the other hand, if your business is one where you hope for repeat business or referrals, don't forget the niceties. Nothing keeps you in a customer's good books as easily as cards for Christmas, birthdays, children's birthdays and other anniversaries. Everyone likes these little gestures, but women are particularly appreciative of them – and sales*men* rarely remember them.

8 Using your head

Women are different from men. I've been telling you that all along, but now it's time to look at why, and how, and what these differences are. Then we can consider how you can better utilise your advantages and minimise some of the self-destructive behaviour that stems from the disadvantages.

Why are we different? Quite simply, because that is the way we have evolved. It is often said that humans are the only creatures on earth that are not specialists – lions have speed and sharp teeth and claws, anteaters have long tongues, spiders have sticky webs and paralysing injections, while we have nothing of this sort. Our teeth are blunt, as are our hands and feet; our outer covering damages easily in the sun, let alone by sharp objects; we can't fly, or even run or swim as well as other beasts. And yet we have made ourselves the lords of creation because we do have a specialisation – a very powerful brain.

The disadvantage of that brain is the time it takes to grow from birth to maturity. Our young are vulnerable for many years, which means that someone has to stay at home looking after them. And this means that someone else has to go out and bring home enough food for everybody. The division of labour fell naturally into the women, who would be either pregnant or nursing, staying close to home gathering small quantities of vegetable food, while the men, unencumbered by children, could go long distances to hunt for large quantities of protein.

This difference in activities led to selective evolutionary differences between the sexes. Men are not only bigger than us, they carry much more muscle and are much stronger. Their upper body is at least twice as powerful, with limbs that throw and carry and heave far better than ours. Their hearts and lungs are larger, and thus can pump more oxygen to their muscles; and they have narrow hips and strong legs which allow them to run further and faster. All these are valuable attributes for pursuing and capturing large animals.

We carry more fat than men, as reserves to keep us and our infants going in lean times. We have wide hips to accommodate babies, shoulders and arms that are adapted for the same purpose and breasts for feeding them, which makes running uncomfortable. We have smaller hands, better adapted to picking fruit and grains than wielding a weapon.

All of this is immediately obvious. What is not so obvious to everyone is that along with the evolution of these physical differences is the evolution of the brain to enable their best use. The brains of men and women also differ in the ways in which they function. This does not mean that men's brains can do things that women's can't, or vice versa, any more than the other specialisations mean that women can't run or men can't do fine fingerwork, but that each sex has developed a brain that tends to be better at some tasks than others.

In order to hunt successfully, men need good control over their large muscles, and good sight. They need to be able to focus quickly at varying distances and they need to make quick calculations of distance, direction and speed. They need the ability to determine a major goal and work out the steps to achieve it, and because such major goals require more than one person to achieve them, they need to be team-oriented. I'll come back to that later, but it must be obvious that you cannot deal with a mammoth on your own!

Women needed fine motor skills for their food-gathering and child-handling and, because they spent most of their time in groups, also needed good social skills. Because they spent time with other people they became concerned about them, which fitted in well with their need to recognise plants and the places where they grew. This would have led to learning the uses of herbs, and it is a reasonable assumption that women were in charge of medicine.

Men had to concentrate on one major task at a time. Daydreaming or admiring the trees when they should have been watching their prey meant everybody going hungry, so they developed a linear method of thinking. Women were more likely to be doing more than one thing at a time – picking fruit, listening for rustles in the undergrowth that might be a tasty mouse or a nasty snake, keeping one eye on the baby and the other on birds who might have a nest of eggs within reach, and all the time deliberating whether to check the nut-trees over the hill or whether it was time to head for home before it got dark. In other words, women developed a more holistic approach to life, and the ability to 'parallel process'.

The brain is rather like half a walnut to look at, with a convoluted surface, and it is divided into two halves, known as hemispheres. We know, from experimental work, and work with people who have suffered from strokes and other forms of brain damage, that certain physiological functions are dealt with by different sides of the brain. We also know that different thinking styles are dealt with in different hemispheres.

The left hemisphere controls the right side of the body,

the right field of vision, the abilty to deal with numbers
and time. It splits information into readily absorbable
chunks and deals with it sequentially. It controls logical
and analytical thought – and it is dominant in most
right-handed males. The right hemisphere controls the
left side of the body, the left field of vision, colour,
language, rhythm and pattern recognition. It controls
intuition and parallel processing – and it is dominant in
most women and a lot of left-handed males.

At this point you may be happy to accept the physiological aspect of all this, but be a little doubtful about
the issue of whether the left or right hemisphere is
dominant in male or female thought processes. (We'll
leave left-handed males out of this; they are a special
case and there is a lot of research currently in progress
on other aspects of their make-up.) Surely, you will be
saying, males or females react the way they do because
that is the way they are traditionally brought up? You
have hit on the 'Nature or Nurture' debate, and the
'Nurture' view so beloved of some feminists, that 'We're
all equal until we're taught to be different', does have a
lot going for it from a logical angle. Alas, Nature has
proved it wrong, for we now know that the differences
are pre-programmed by chromosomes and hormones,
and they can be detected in the unborn foetus.

So there it is. Brain function is a product of gender.
The problem, as far as we are concerned, is that in our
male-dominated Western culture, the faculties associated with the left brain – rationality, logic, analytical
thinking and a linear approach to problems – are considered more valuable than the creative, intuitive right-
brain approach.

The more you work in a male-dominated environment,
the more you will try to submerge your feminine right-

brain characteristics – your empathic sensitivity, your general interest in people, your intuition. And you mustn't, or you will end up in dreadful paralysing conflict with yourself. Fortunately, it is not a total 'either/or' situation. It does tend to be so for many men, but women are generally better able to integrate their left and right brains than men. We are less lateralised, and this shows clearly in all the tests used to show left/right differences.

This means that we can adopt as many of the left-brain characteristics as we need for our current situation without having to submerge totally the right-brain approach. Oddly enough, a very high proportion of ultra-successful men place a high value on their intuition. They don't call it that – 'intuition' is all too often preceded by the dread tag 'feminine', so they make it more acceptable and macho by calling it a hunch or a gut feeling. Others say they like to 'sleep on it' and trust the answer they wake up with. You've probably found yourself that it often produces the perfect solution to a problem.

What this means is that the right brain is beavering away on its own, whether or not you are aware of it. Just because the conscious mode of thought is of the left-brain analytical variety, it doesn't mean that the 'unconscious' other half is doing nothing. The stars are there all the time – we just can't see them during the day because the sun is too bright. But when night comes, if you turn off the lights, they shine out in all their glory.

Learn to trust your intuition. It is every bit as valid, and every bit as based on informational input, as your so-called logical thought processes. There are a couple of ways you can help it along. The first is transcendental meditation. EEG studies of TM practitioners show increased interaction between the two hemispheres.

The other way is to practise recalling your dreams, by writing down what you remember of them as soon as you wake up. Dreams are dealt with by the right brain, but many ultra-logical people (accountants, actuaries, lawyers etc.) have such a dominant left brain that they will tell you they do not dream at all. They do. We all do, but they have lost their ability to recall their dreams.

You should not only learn how to get in touch with your intuition, it is also sensible to work out the other ways in which your brain functions and encourage them rather than fight them.

Probably the most important of these functions is your ability to learn and memorise. Even if you elect to remain in one industry all your working life, there will always be new developments and new products to learn about, and new customers who will expect you to remember what they have told you about themselves.

Although learning and memorising aren't quite the same thing, they are closely linked, especially where facts are concerned. We *learn* physical skills, but once we have learned them, we do not have to consciously *remember* how to do them, for our kinesthetic memory takes over and turns them into automatic muscular routines. Once you have learned to ride a bicycle, for instance, you just get on it and ride it without having to tell the different parts of your body how to deal with pedals, handlebars, balance etc. You will find that this applies to the physical aspects of your presentations, from handling the product itself to operating an overhead projector. This is, of course, why you should rehearse your routines so that you are body perfect as well as word perfect. Then you will safely be able to leave the mechanical aspects to your kinesthetic memory, so the rest of your head is free to concentrate on audience feedback.

There are two areas of factual learning you have to deal with – the hard and unyielding technical facts about your product, and the subjective and objective facts about your customers. The same principles apply to learning both. Take the subject matter in small chunks, and review what you have studied at regular intervals. Where the subjective aspects are concerned, this principle becomes 'review, and amend your first impressions'.

By 'subjective' I mean both the things the customers have told you about themselves and the things you have deduced about them from your own observations. You should always take everything people tell you about themselves with a pinch of salt. There is nothing as self-deluding as a human being – you only have to look at the clothes half of them wear to realise that they see themselves in a totally different light from the way other people see them. Even what they tell you about their businesses will be the way they see it rather than the way it really is. (The bankruptcy statistics are clear proof of this!)

Your own deductions about them, particularly those based on the techniques in Chapter Four, must certainly be reviewed. The person you interpreted as a particularly defensive, difficult man may be a perfectly mild-mannered man who has just had an acrimonious encounter with a traffic warden. Next time you see him, he will be back to normal, but if you are treating him with kid gloves he may decide that this is because you have something to hide.

You may be new to these techniques and have missed some of the clues. Experience will soon solve that problem and, as with riding a bicycle, you will find that you can absorb the whole instead of having to deal with the individual parts (right brain again). This comes under the heading of pattern recognition and it is one of the major factors that makes the difference between a superbly successful salesperson and a mediocre one.

The ability to recognise a significant pattern, whether it be in a prospect's behaviour or in a physical situation, such as the position of the pieces on a chessboard, is a valuable short cut to critical path analysis. To stay with the chess analogy, just think of the thought processes involved in deciding your move. 'If I move my bishop to there, he could move his queen to there, and unless I then move my knight there, he could . . .' You can keep this up for hours, but what distinguishes Grand Masters from other players is their ability to look at the board and think, 'This is the classic Bloggski position which I encountered last year in Moscow; what I did then was this successful move', instead of going through all that 'If . . . then . . .' stuff. In a selling situation, it is a collection of subtle clues about the prospect that tells you whether you are on to a sale or encountering resistance masked by politeness.

What is actually happening here is that you have taken a 'chunk' of information and given it a label. By labelling that chunk of information, you make access to all its component parts and the most appropriate responses that much easier.

This ability to 'chunk' information comes, of course, from experience. Before you have gained that experience you need to do some critical path analysis, as you do in all new situations. This is also known as 'decision tree' thinking and is the most valuable thinking habit you can learn. It is the thing that separates not only successful and mediocre salespeople, but outstanding and mediocre people in all walks of life. I know I keep on about this separation, but it is very important. If you do not consider situations properly, you cannot reach sensible decisions and you cannot take positive actions. It is a common female trait to wait for things to happen, to drift with the tide and hope for the best instead of taking action to ensure the outcome we want. Everything comes to she who waits? Does it hell! If you want something, you have to learn to take control of your life to make things happen. Never mind the fairy tales about Cinderella or Sleeping Beauty, where the Princess is recognised and given her due reward – if you want success, you have to go get it for yourself.

This does not mean that you should jump in with your eyes shut, under the impression that you are taking action. That is not action, it is reaction without thought – and it leads to disaster more often than success. A few minutes' consideration along the 'If ... then ...' lines will provide a better route than, 'Here we go, it's bound to be all right.' It will at least give you an idea of the risks and rewards inherent in each choice of action. All you have to do then is decide whether the rewards attract you more than the risks repel you.

This is another of the differences between the sexes. It is a product of an earlier evolutionary stage, but it still applies today. Men see risk as part of the process leading to reward, and take it in their stride – hunting mammoths is dangerous, but if you get one it will see several families through the winter. Women see risk as totally negative and something to be avoided. This is almost certainly because of the relative values of the rewards available to male and female activities. A handful of nuts is not worth the hazard of damaging yourself – which means not only your own life, but probably the life of your young child and your current foetus. Now that we are operating in a world where the rewards are equal for both sexes, however, we must learn to consider risk in a less negative light.

All of this has taken us a long way from the processes of learning and memorising. Most of the vocal and visual input you get from customers will come in small, easy-to-absorb chunks, but you may need to learn large amounts of technical data about their requirements as well as about your own products. With this, break it into chunks yourself, or break your learning periods up into short spells. Half an hour's concentrated study at a time is plenty, then you should take a short break. Get up and walk about, have a cup of coffee, if possible go outside for a breath of fresh air, then you will be able to absorb another chunk of information. Start each study period by reviewing what you already know. You will find that you remember more of what you were learning when you go back after a break than you did when you stopped for the break. This applies to learning a physical skill as well – your right brain is getting to work while your left brain is thinking about that coffee.

Do make sure that you keep reviewing what has gone before. With the advantage of your most recent knowledge, the early information will fall into place and be retained better. For this reason, if you are having trouble with a particular aspect, leave it and come back to it later, when it will probably make more sense.

When it comes to figures, very few people can hold more than nine numbers in their memory. Seven is the norm, which is why most of us have little difficulty with telephone numbers. With the longer numbers, it helps to use the old name of the exchange, because that puts a chunk of the number under another label. I have no difficulty over such numbers as my favourite Chinese restaurant – 0959 62005 – because I think of it as Westerham 62005, then remember that Westerham is 0959. Most part numbers for car spares are seven-figure numbers, or a combination of small groups of letters and numbers, and the same grouping system applies throughout industry. If you need to memorise such numbers for your products, look for a way to connect them with some other meaningful number – your birthdate, your car number, a silly rhyme (One, two, three, Mother caught a flea!') or the Bingo calls (Legs – eleven; Two fat ladies – eighty-eight') – anything that fixes them in your head.

The same techniques apply with names or other bits of information. Put a silly picture together to describe a name and you will never forget it (Mr Pearson – a small boy peering through a crack in a door; or Mr Clutter-buck – a large male rabbit sitting in a shed full of clutter), or see if you can work out a mnemonic for it. Which of these is easier to remember: 'Don't complicate the issue, or your audience will be confused' or 'KISS? Keep It Simple, Stupid!' The more unusual and out-rageous your pictures or mnemonics, the better you will remember them.

Many people say they have difficulty in remembering names, but this is usually for the simple reason that they weren't paying attention when they were introduced. Forgetting a prospect's name is probably the best way to blow your chances of a sale, so if you have this tendency, you will have to make a conscious effort to cure yourself. When you are introduced to someone, repeat the name back to them – 'How do you do, Mr White?' – and try to find some way of commenting on the name to fix it in your mind. 'Is that White with an I, or with a Y?' 'Jones –

are you actually from Wales?' Nobody ever minds talking about their name, as long as you aren't smart-alecky about it, and the longer you discuss it, the more likely you will be to remember it.

This principle also applies to that tricky technical data. Don't struggle to understand it on your own. Talk it over with your colleagues. They will probably have had trouble with the same things, and they may be able to give you their own formulae for remembering.

It won't do you any harm to select a mentor from among your colleagues. A mentor is a person with more experience than you, who is prepared to accept you as a disciple and guide your progress. Mentors can be of either sex, but since women with extensive selling experience are still comparatively rare, you will probably have to choose a man.

You may be wondering why you need a mentor when your boss is supposed to help you, but they are not the same. If your boss is any good at his job, it is because he is a manager rather than a salesman. The two beasts do not necessarily occupy the same skin, but even if they do, the sales activities must be restricted by the need to manage. What you need is someone who is still actively selling, who has his finger on the pulse of the job. You also need someone with whom you can discuss your boss and how he might react to your style and ideas. What has just struck you as a brilliant innovation may have been tried in the past and failed. Wouldn't you rather know that fact before you go bouncing in to see the boss, all bright-eyed and bushy-tailed?

In case you are thinking that there is something underhand about seeking this sort of help, and that you should go it alone, let me tell you that it is a situation that men take for granted. It is part of that team mentality I mentioned earlier, which has developed from the hunting band to a sporting group. Boys are brought up playing sports that have a very heavy emphasis on teams. This can produce some very odd attitudes, such as the way they are prepared to tolerate a total incompetent whom we think ought to be fired. What they can see is that with him, useless though he is, they have a full team. Without him, they wouldn't have a full team and that means they couldn't play at all.

Although each member of the team values his team position, he would also like to be the star who scores the goals. This helps the team as well as him, and he therefore considers it legitimate – nay, laudable – that he should get some extra coaching by finding a mentor to help him. So your conscience can be quite clear.

It is unlikely that you will find the experience you need in someone of your own generation, so you should look for an older man. That should allow you to fall into a father/daughter type relationship, which is by far the safest, where you, he and his wife are concerned. Not that you need expect to get involved with their family life, but if you want the man's help it is hardly fair to complicate his life by letting his wife think that you are up to mischief together.

And you won't be, will you? Not with your mentor, or anyone else on the team. You are there to work, remember, not to get laid. That won't do your reputation any good at all. The double standard still exists where morality is concerned – you will be thought of as 'easy', and it will be assumed that your judgement in other areas is also at fault. It will also be suggested, possibly to your face, that your sales are obtained either as handouts from the boss for favours received, or as responses from customers for the same favours. *You* know that it's the equipment between your ears that matters, not the equipment between your legs, but the suggestions can be very hurtful.

It is bad enough worrying about what you will do when a prospect tells you he'll buy if you go to bed with him. There is no point in worrying about this, however. It may never happen, but if it does, all you can do is say, 'Thanks, but no thanks,' and get out with as much of your dignity as you can. There is no need to say any more, except perhaps a heartfelt 'Pervert!' as you pass his secretary. (She probably knows anyway, poor girl.) You may also like to mentally rehearse some diversion routines, like tipping coffee over his desk and onto his lap, to keep him occupied while you make your escape.

This rehearsal of possible difficult situations is the only way you will be able to keep your cool. There are customers who will pull nasty tricks to try and get an advantage out of you, and jealous colleagues who will deliberately needle you in the hope that they can make you feel small. These are the ones who love to crow, 'Emotional woman!', and you need to practise some cutting remarks to put them back in their place instead of getting angry and bursting into tears.

Think of all the situations that might make you react that way. Then run through them step by step in your head as many times as it takes to get to the end without feeling upset. This will help, but it will not be foolproof, especially if one of these attacks (don't kid yourself that they are anything else) is launched at you when you are due for a period. All you can do in that situation is to recognise the early-warning signs of tears and seize any available excuse to get away on your own until you have regained control. Sipping cold water is very therapeutic, and teabags dipped in cold water are excellent for taking the redness away from your eyes.

You are less likely to be attacked in this way if your general image is one of self control. Don't set yourself up by using nervous gestures or emotive language like, 'I can't stand it.' Remember your body language, and exude serenity and confidence by smiling calmly and staying very still. The needlers will soon find that it is no fun baiting you, and they'll go away and leave you in peace to get on with your job.

9 Using your time

I have already suggested that you should cost your time to see whether you are spending your own high-value time on the low-value task of basic prospecting. Having established that time values can vary, let's consider some other ways of saving your high-value time for high-value tasks.

The obvious first step has to be to delegate as much as you can to someone else. There is a hazard in this, in that it is easy to imagine that delegation means dumping all the nasty jobs. If you do that, you will soon find yourself short of a helper, for even low-paid workers need job satisfaction. Nor does it mean that you should expect these jobs to be done exactly as you used to do them, or that you should get constant blow-by-blow reports on what is being done. That takes almost as long to oversee as it would to do the job yourself. The whole idea of delegation is to find someone you can trust to do the job properly, then let them do it their way. Otherwise you will be forever stuck at the level of what you can actually do yourself instead of what you can control.

You will obviously need to do a certain amount of training before you can totally relinquish each task. Do be sure that you explain not only what you want done, but why, or you risk false assumptions causing misdirection errors. Be clear on parameters – there is a vast difference between appointments in South Wales and appointments within a twenty-mile radius of Cardiff. Adopt a rule of 'only report results that require me to act', and then trust that report. If you are given a list of appointments in a certain area, don't drop in on another prospect just because you are passing. It could well be one of the refusals or, worse yet, a prospect your assistant has just spoken to. If the result was an appointment for tomorrow, you have just made yourself look totally disorganised.

If what you have is a general assistant or secretary, rather than someone hired to do a specific task, make sure that they have sufficient intelligence and education to be really useful rather than just a defence line between you and the rest of the world. What you want is someone who can deal with telephone queries instead of just taking messages, and who can write decent business letters instead of just taking dictation.

And don't be mean. If your assistant has helped you pull off a big deal, or with a bumper year's production, this deserves a decent remuneration and a bonus. I know of a pair of life assurance salesmen who shared an assistant. He made all their appointments for them, dealt with all their paperwork and correspondence, and even wrote long technical reports for them. He worked a good forty-hour week for them, for which they each gave him £60 a week. He has just woken up to the fact that they are earning over £100,000 a year each – and quit. They are currently doing a good imitation of headless chickens because they can't get a replacement.

Once you have unburdened yourself of all the tasks which someone else could do, it is time to examine the tasks that are left, to see what you can ditch, permanently. Of course you can't abandon the things you need to do to keep customers happy, but it is always worth examining your internal reporting tasks.

Ask the recipients of your routine returns whether they really need them. You may be spending your precious time preparing reports on your activities that they no longer need at all, or only need once a year instead of every month. Don't assume that they would tell you if this was the case – some junior clerk at head office may be assiduously filing your pieces of paper in case his boss needs them one day, while the boss has forgotten that they ever existed.

The next line of thought is the one that comes under the banner of 'who pays for lunch?'. The answer to this question is, of course, 'He who stands to gain most from it', which allows you to label tasks 'I want' or 'they want'. From there, it's easy. You do the 'I want' tasks; they do the 'they want' tasks!

The final question is whether you are spending too much time on alligators. ('When you are up to your neck in alligators, it is difficult to remember that you are meant to be draining the swamp.') It is amazing how much time you can spend in apologising for, or covering up for, things you have omitted to do, when actually doing those things would have taken very little time anyway.

So if you are not doing the things you should be doing, how are you spending your time? That is not a rhetorical question, but part of a valuable exercise. Take a piece of paper and list, half an hour at a time, just how you have spent your time for the last week. Not just your working time, but every half hour of the whole day. Then, every day for a further week, list what you have done. If you went to bed at ten o'clock, read till one-thirty, and woke up at eight o'clock, list this as six and a half hours sleeping and three and a half hours reading. Reading what? A novel or the operating manual on your new product? List them separately and don't cheat, on this or any other aspect of your day. Nobody is going to see this except you, and there is no point in fooling yourself.

Then put those lists to one side, and on a fresh piece of paper write down all the things you think you ought to be doing, whether or not you are, and reorganise this list in order of importance. Then take the list of what you were actually doing, reorganise it according to the time spent on each activity, and compare it with the list of desirable activities. When you have recovered from the shock of realising how much time you spend on low-priority activities (and sleep and recreation should *not* be low on your 'desirable' list) you are ready for the rest of the exercise.

Give yourself ten minutes to write down the answers to these two questions. 'What do I really want to do with my life? What do I want to be able to look back on proudly as achievements when I am on my deathbed?' Don't try to make value judgements on your answers, just list them as they come to you. Want to be rich and famous? Write romantic novels? Walk up Everest? Knit a million woolly hats for Oxfam? Write them all down, and when your time is up, rearrange them in order of importance.

Now spend ten minutes listing all the things you want to achieve in the next three years; then rearrange that in order of importance. Then compare those two lists. This should allow you to refine the possibilities from the daydreams in the first list.

The next question is this. If you had just been told that you only had six months to live, how would you spend them? This may seem an odd question, especially since many of your answers to the previous questions will have been work-oriented, and no one with any sense spends their last months working. But if these are things that you want to do that much, why aren't you doing some of them now?

There are three possible answers to that. Your relation-ship with someone is preventing you, or you can't afford it, or you haven't got time. The financial problem is, we hope, going to be cured as a result of reading this book. As for the relationship problem, ask yourself this ques-tion: if spending time with that person is so important, why isn't it a prominent feature on your 'before I die' list instead of an obstacle?

The time problem can be cured if you invest a little of the time you think you haven't got in reorganising your-self to use all your time in the best possible way, which is the purpose behind all this list-making. Once you know what you want to do, you can make some realistic plans to help you do it, without going up blind alleys en route.

There are two ways of making better use of your time, and each has its devotees. There is no reason why you should not combine the two, if that works for you. The first involves allocating chunks of time for specific tasks. Rule a piece of paper up for seven days, split it into half hours, and make some copies. Add dates from now as far ahead as you can. Then, using a set of coloured pens or highlighters, block in different colours for dif-ferent activities. You will have to refer to your appoint-ment diary for a lot of this, but do try to organise it so you do each thing at the same time each day.

Just do one week at first, then consult your chart each day to see what you should be doing that day, and how far you deviated from yesterday's plan. Mark it with ticks or crosses, then when you do next week's plan you can take these deviations into account. Once you have had a few weeks' practice, you will find that you can start filling in blocks several weeks ahead.

Don't forget to take your monthly cycle into con-sideration. If you habitually spend the days just before your period snarling at people, allocate those days to non-stressful routine tasks, and reallocate the stressful tasks to days when you will be better able to cope with them. The same applies to your daily cycle. You may not have registered it as such, but we all have regular ups and downs. Observe yourself for a while to map your cycle, then allocate alert times to difficult jobs and dull times to breaks for coffee or fresh air. If these dull times don't respond to short breaks or changes of activity, ask yourself if your eating habits are meeting your body's blood sugar needs, or if you need more sleep.

Or maybe you are sleeping too much. There is a school of thought that says we don't actually need eight hours' sleep. Certainly a lot of successful people say they sleep for no more than five hours, which gives them three more useful hours in each day.

Where you make regular calls to the same customers, try to work out their daily cycle and the times when they are most receptive. If you devise a system of marks to indicate the result of each call you make, you will eventually be able to check this out. (You will also be able to see whether your own success rate varies with the time of day.) When your regular customer is a woman, you should also be alert for clues to her menstrual cycle and what it does to her temper.

The other way of ensuring that you make better use of your time is a system of priorities. Only you can decide exactly what your priorities are, but there are a few ground rules to help you with those decisions.

Look to the future rather than the past. Unless you have a desperate need to prevent some authority catching up with you, you will gain little benefit from dwelling on history. Keep your thoughts firmly on opportunities to come, but always with due attention to their potential.

That will allow you to choose the directions that will really make a difference, especially if you remember the 80/20 rule.

This rule crops up in all sorts of ways, but the one that applies here is that 20 per cent of your customers will probably produce 80 per cent of your sales. This means that you need to work out who that 20 per cent are and concentrate on them. You do need to be ruthless about this. There is no point in spending a week interviewing a prospect and preparing lengthy reports for him if you know the best result will be a sale worth no more than £50 in commission, unless he really is the only customer in town. £50 is better than nothing, but it is not as good as £500.

What you do is to go back to making lists, but very specific ones. Instead of a vague 'write letters', you put 'write to head office re invoices, Mrs Higgins follow-up, John Doe re car' etc. These are called 'to do' lists, and they can be very satisfying, because when you have done each thing, you cross it off your list. But there's a fly in the ointment — because it is so nice to cross things off your list, there is a great temptation to do all the easy things first. And the easy things have a tendency not to be the important ones.

So what you should do is list everything, then go through the list and mark each task A, B, C or Z. If you like lists, you can then indulge yourself by reorganising it into separate lists of each category. A is for the urgent tasks which you must do today, B for the not quite so desperate ones that will wait till tomorrow, C for those that could wait until next week, and Z for the ones that would be nice to do but are not essential. Then you go through the A list and mark all those in order of priority — A1, A2, A3 etc. There is no need to do this with the Bs or

Cs, as they either become As or fade into Zs. Zs you move on to someone else, or throw out completely. This last technique is known in my office as 'round filing', or 'binning'.

If you don't care for lists, you can jot each job down on a 3" by 5" file card and juggle these into order of importance. On the whole, though, lists are easier to carry with you in a notebook or Filofax, because one major aspect of all this is that you must get into the habit of writing down each 'I must do . . .' thought as it comes to you. If it's on a list, your head can discard it and use that bit of brain space for something else.

You need to consult the list at regular intervals to see what to do next and check your priorities. Some people prefer to do this as part of their winding-down process at the end of the day, others like to do it first thing in the morning when they are fresh. But the point of the whole thing is that you never do a C job unless there really is nothing you can do on As or Bs, and you don't do Bs when you could be doing an A. If you find you are putting off an A on the grounds that it will take a longer block of time than you have available now, split it up into smaller tasks that you have got time for.

It is in any case a good idea to split tasks up into small units, and organise them in such a way that you can carry what you need to do them with you when you leave the office. (I keep a plastic folder in my briefcase with little jobs in it.) Then, if you have to wait to see your customer, or have a cancelled appointment in the middle of the day, you can use that spare time for something constructive instead of thumb-twiddling. And even better, you get the reward of crossing something off your list instead of feeling guilty for wasting time.

You do feel guilty when you waste time, don't you? You

should, it's a finite resource. It is very easy to convince yourself that time-wasting is really something else, but the end product is the same — if you weren't spending that time on a productive task, you were wasting it. Incidentally, don't fall into the classic trap of telling yourself that you are relaxing when you are just gawping blankly into space. Relaxing is another matter, and we'll deal with it later.

One of the worst time-wasters is an inability to make decisions. It is by no means an exclusively female problem. Lots of men suffer from it as well, but with them it tends to stem from fear of the consequences of a wrong decision, while with us it is more likely to be lack of practice. Of course we suffer from the fear of failure too, but the answer to that is to realise that we do not have to be perfect. Nobody can be right all the time. If only half of your decisions turn out to have been right, you are performing averagely, so if you are right on more than half, you are above average. The way to improve your hit rate is to make considered decisions rather than blind jumps at options.

Work your way through this set of questions. What do I want to achieve? How many ways are there to achieve it? Do I have all the information I need to assess these? Can I reject any immediately as being impractical or too costly? Which will bring the highest benefit? Which will create the worst problems if it is the wrong decision? Are any of these problems so bad that they should not be risked? What will happen if I don't make a decision at all?

Then go back to the first question and try looking at it from another angle in case you have fallen into the trap of assuming rigid parameters that don't exist. There is a theory that says our brains operate like a blancmange with hot sauce being poured on it. Once the first lot of sauce has melted pathways down the sides of the blancmange, any more sauce tends to follow the same paths, making them deeper, instead of cutting new routes to the bottom.

Try this little exercise. Give yourself two minutes to write down all the things you can do with a brick, then count them. Most people come up with a lot of variations on two basic uses – building-material or missile, and stop at that. The best list I've seen had twenty completely different ones, and it included foot-warmer (after a spell in the oven), ashtray, ruler and knife-sharpener.

Once you have considered all the options, you can make a decision on the best of the alternatives. Because that is what decisions are – choosing from alternatives. And if you know why you made your decision, you will make a better one next time, especially if you take the sensible course of de-briefing yourself afterwards – identifying the reasons why what you decided turned out right or wrong.

Another of the classic time-wasters is meetings. I don't mean meetings with customers, but the ones in your own company. It is not easy to avoid them if your boss wants you there and you don't have a solid appointment with a genuine customer (you'd better come back with an order!). Nor is it possible to control them unless you are in the chair, but you might be able to shorten them a bit by judicious use of the phrase, 'Aren't we getting away from the point?'

This applies to formal meetings, but impromptu ones can be just as bad. If you get called in to one, you can set your own parameters by stating, 'I can only give you ten minutes,' then keep checking your watch. If they come to you, you can say the same thing, but you can also stand up, which keeps them on their feet; refuse to indulge in the social chit-chat which only prolongs the interruption; learn to make short non-committal responses to complaints about things that are not your fault, instead of indulging the complainer with the sympathy they desire; and, most importantly of all, develop the art of terminating conversations. Some people have great difficulty in doing this, and stand around going 'Um . . . er . . .' In this situation there is nothing for it but to take charge and say firmly, 'OK, then, we'll do that. Thank you.' Then you turn away and go back to whatever you were doing before.

Another common waste of time is reading the newspapers, with the rationalisation that they may contain something relevant to your job. The fact of the matter is that they rarely do. Your reading time would be better spent on trade magazines or technical books. If you feel that this would take too much time, you may think of learning to speed read. The principle behind this is that you should take in blocks of print, rather than try to read every word. You don't move your eyes across each line, but straight down the middle of the page. Your peripheral vision should take in everything up to the margins, instead of being wasted on blank paper, as it is when you scan back and forth. Use a timer as a training aid. See how much you can read in ten minutes, then try to increase that amount each day. It doesn't count if you don't take in what you have read, but you will soon find that your eye will latch on to significant words and draw your attention to that passage.

Even if you do speed read (and most people who take the courses fail to maintain their new speed unless they practise every day) you are still risking information overload. This can make you conclude that you will never be able to learn it all and give up reading altogether. It is better to read selectively. There is no reason why you should read the whole of a book, especially a technical one. Read the blurb, look at the index to see how detailed it is, then look at the table of contents to see which chapters you need to read now. Glance through them first to see if they really are relevant, and then you can actually read them if you need to.

Apart from not wasting it, there are a lot of ways in which you can actually save time. The main one is streamlining your handling of paper. Don't walk about opening your mail, sit at your desk and deal with each item as you open it, rather than reading it and putting it in a pile, then having to go through the pile handling each piece of paper a second time. If someone else can deal with it, redirect it, making any notes for their guidance on the back. With internal memos, hand write your response on them, photocopy and send them off instead of generating another piece of paper by dictating a reply. Enlightened offices have NCR (no carbon required) memo pads for this purpose. The new sticky notelets are also marvellous.

Be ruthless with rubbish. As soon as you have recognised it as such, throw it away instead of cluttering your desk with it. If for some reason you can't act on a piece of paper, put it in a 'bring forward' file rather than a pending tray, but date each item and leave them until then, rather than having to wade through the whole pile every day to get to the ones you can do. And with every piece of paper that remains when you have done all that, you write A, B or C.

Probably one of the best ways to save time is to plan your day so that you do the things everyone has to do at times when they don't. Travel outside the rush hour –

whichever way you travel, it is faster and more comfort-able. If you have to shop, or get lunch, do that early or late, too, rather than stand in queues. Have your hair done in the middle of the week instead of Friday after-noon. If you have to make personal appointments with such people as the dentist, ask them when is the best time for a quick turn-round. And if they do keep you waiting, don't just sit there patiently for hours. If you have allocated a reasonable length of time for the appointment and you are still waiting when that time is up, tell the receptionist you cannot wait any longer and make another appointment. If they do it to you a second time, change your dentist!

Invest some time in organising your files so that you can go straight to what you want. Label them clearly – don't rely on your memory. Filing materials are so cheap that it is silly not to use them to ease your work. The same goes for a lot of other mechanical aids.

Dictating-machines don't keep you waiting while they sharpen their pencils. You can use them anywhere, any time you have five minutes, and post the tapes back to base so that letters are ready for signing when you get back. If you have to do your own typing, get a word processor and learn to use standard phrases in your correspondence.

Get a Filofax or some other ring binder, so you have everything you need in one place – diary, addresses and phone numbers, 'to do' lists etc. Carry stamped or reply paid envelopes to get material back to the office every day. Get a modern telephone and make use of all its facilities – directory memory, one-button redial, 'hands off' mode. But unless the company is paying for it, think hard and long before getting a car or mobile phone. The effective ones are *very* expensive, both to acquire (buy or lease) and to make calls on. For most people they are an indulgence rather than an essential piece of equipment, and you could save a couple of thousand a year by doing without.

It is also sensible to let whoever deals with your messages know where you are going to be at any given time; then if anything urgent crops up they know where to find you. Make sure they realise that your day's calls have been organised to take the least travelling time between each one, and that you won't deviate from that route for anything less than a really urgent matter (make sure their definition of 'really urgent' is the same as yours). It is worth using pins and string on a map to work out the best route round your calls, but if you are driving, do check the road reports on the radio before you commit yourself to a particular road.

There's nothing like traffic jams to make you late for an appointment – and nothing like being late for destroying your credibility with a customer.

10 Coping at home

Using your time wisely should not just apply to your working time, but to your private life as well – not that it is always easy to draw the line in a selling job. It is a basic fact of working life that the more money you earn, the less likely you are to leave the office at five p.m. and give your job no more thought until nine a.m. the next day. With selling, even if the product does not require evening visits to customers, you will often find yourself travelling outside normal office hours or attending conferences and other business meetings.

You will therefore soon find that you have less time available for your domestic and social life, which makes it all the more important that none of that time is wasted. It is easy enough to define wasted time at work – time spent during the working day which does not move the job on in one way or another. But surely you need relaxation time at home? By all means – but there are also things which need to be done to keep life running smoothly, and if you deal with these tasks in an efficient manner you will have all the more time for true relaxation.

Probably the worst time-waster in the modern world is the television. People often ask me how I find time to research and write books, as well as run a full-time job, a house and my social life. My answer is always the same – we do not have a television. This can lead to some interesting encounters with the licence people, who cannot understand how anyone can live without the rubbish that comprises 95 per cent of programmes, but even they have finally accepted that we haven't got one.

It is five years now since we lived in a house with a television, and we don't miss it at all. On the rare occasions when there is a programme we really want to see, we go and watch it at my mother's. That happens about twice a month, but the rest of the time we do perfectly well without it. Do yourselves a favour and get rid of yours, or at the very least get a video and tape the programmes you think you can't live without, then watch them when it suits you instead of when it suits the schedulers. That way you won't get trapped into watching the next programme as well.

The same thing applies to the radio. Most programmes are time-killers, or deal with their subject in a manner designed to cater for the lowest common denominator, so you can't even claim that you are educating yourself by listening to it while doing your housework. What you are actually doing is filling your head with 'noise', which prevents your brain from doing what it should while your body performs simple mechanical tasks – either planning ahead or letting your right brain work on your current problems.

Another major time-waster at home is unexpected visitors. Salespeople are bad enough. At least one has a certain amount of sympathy with someone who is trying to earn a living (not too much sympathy – if you can do it without door-knocking, so can they). The really annoying ones are charity collectors (why should you be expected to give to *every* 'good cause'?) and the political or religious pests who want to force their opinions on you. The only answer to these intrusions is blatant rudeness. You may find it difficult the first time, telling someone, 'Four letter off, I'm busy!' but you'll be delighted at how effective it is.

The other answer is not to go to the door at all. Either install an entry-phone, which itself repels most of these pests, or copy the lady I read about who had a sign on her door that said, 'The bell has been disconnected. If you are expected, knock. If not, don't bother. I won't answer!'

The same rule applies to the telephone. Get an answering machine, and never actually answer the phone yourself unless you are expecting a specific call. Genuine callers will leave a message, and the nuisances – heavy breathers as well as double-glazing salesmen – will hang up.

Just as bad as the salespeople and preachers are the friends and acquaintances who drop in whenever it suits them. Since you have probably encouraged them in the past to think that they are welcome by abandoning what you were doing to attend to them, it probably never occurs to them that they are not always welcome. But uninvited visitors really are an intrusion, and you will have to retrain your friends if you are to get full control of your own time.

It is actually quite easy to do this. You greet them on the doorstep with, 'Oh dear, what a pity you didn't phone first, I could have saved you a wasted journey.' You don't actually need to say any more than that, as long as you don't weaken and add, 'Oh well, since you're here you might as well come in for a few minutes.' If you must make an excuse as to why you are not going to invite them in (and there's no reason why you should – it's *your* home), you have a choice between, 'I'm just getting ready to go out,' 'I'm in the middle of a report for tomorrow's meeting and I daren't stop,' or 'I think I'm coming down with flu.'

With the ones who do ring to say they were thinking of

popping in, you say, 'Oh, dear, what a pity, I would have loved to see you. Why don't you ring me next week and we'll make a date to get together properly.' They will soon get the message that the only way to get your attention is to arrange a time in advance.

Once you have your friends trained, you are freed from the necessity to keep yourself and your home immaculate all the time. You can have a grand clean-up when visitors are due, but the rest of the time you can leave it to settle into whatever level of tidiness you like yourself. If you are a real slob, arrange to meet your friends somewhere else and make it clear to lovers that they provide the bed. Then all you have to worry about is keeping your clothes and your body in good order, and you can shut the door on the rest. Keeping your body in good order requires a certain standard of kitchen hygiene as well as decent bathing facilities, but there is no life rule that says your private dwelling space has to be like the glossy magazines, or that you have to provide Cordon Bleu meals for your fellow dwellers every night of the week.

If you do want to live like that, your best bet is to pay someone to do it for you. Either find someone to come in on an hourly basis, or go to your local housework franchise and get them to do it for you. I have tried both, and they both have their merits. A personal arrangement with an individual is by far the cheapest, but it is not always easy to find and keep the right person. Franchises cost more, but they do vet their staff, carry insurance against breakages and theft and relieve you of such nasty tasks as dealing with alcoholics who cannot resist the temptation of your booze cupboard. This happened to me – she was a lovely lady and did a superb job most of the time, but when we came home two days running to find her in a drunken stupor on our bed, she had to go. There were no horrid confrontations. We just rang the franchise and said we'd like someone else, thank you.

Whichever way you do it, it is essential that they understand exactly what you want done. If you are not into housework yourself, it is tempting to say, 'It's all yours, just get on with it,' but experience has taught me that it is much better to say (or leave a note saying), 'Today I want you to iron shirts, then hoover round, and if you've got any time left, change the beds.'

If you can't afford to pay someone, or you don't care for the idea of someone in your house when you are not there, you'll have to do it yourself. The first thing is to decide what you really do and don't need to do. Then you can work out the best ways to do the essentials and maybe even rearrange the environment to make it all easier. If you live with other people, they should be involved in this planning and you should all decide what share of the work you will each do.

That means everybody. Even small children can do their bit by putting toys away and taking responsibility for certain items. No one can call it slave labour for a five-year-old to collect old newspapers and put them in a box in the kitchen, or to collect dirty socks and put them in the laundry basket. Anyone who is old enough to be trusted with a vacuum cleaner does their own room, makes their own bed and looks after their own clothes. Teach everyone to put things away by collecting stray items and dumping them in a box, then put the box out for the dustmen. And teach them to think ahead by refusing to cooperate in early morning 'I haven't got a clean football shirt!' panics. It'll be hell at the time, but it will only happen once.

Dispense with sheets and blankets and get duvets

instead. Redecorate with wipe-down surfaces and colours or patterns that disguise grubby marks. Invest in matting inside doors that removes muck from the shoes, or instigate a 'slippers only' rule indoors. Don't choose dark colours for your bathroom suite, especially if you live in a hard-water area. They are impossible to keep mark-free.

If you have room, put the washing machine and dryer in the bathroom, so clothes can go straight from bodies into the machine. Buy a second hoover for upstairs, and keep other cleaning items in various places round the house instead of lugging them up and down all the time. Or get pinafores with big kangaroo pockets to hold cleaning materials and to collect items that have strayed out of place.

Go for maximum automation in the kitchen, but do think when buying gadgets about how long they will take to disassemble and wash. There is no point in using a food processor to grate a piece of cheese if it then takes twenty minutes to clean it. Don't be seduced into buying gadgets until you have talked to friends who have them to find out if they are really useful. We have a microwave oven, but I rarely use it to cook in. I use it for de-frosting, warming hard butter, reheating coffee and providing luxurious hot flannels. It is actually easier to cook on the hob or in a conventional oven.

By far the most useful gadgets I have are the slow cooker and the deep freeze. You can buy vegetables and meat ready prepared to dump in the slow cooker before you leave in the morning and it lurks there all day on 'low' until you come home to eat it – or rather, eat half of it and freeze the rest for another time. If your crockery is freezer/oven/microwave/dishwasher proof, you don't even have to change dishes.

If you have children, teach them to cook as soon as they are old enough. Let each one prepare supper on one set day each week. If they have a cookery class at school, that will be the most suitable day, but if not they will soon fall into the routine and be proud to do it. You do not do children any favours by waiting on them as they grow up. They would far rather be involved in the family at all levels, which means at decision level too. If you get the whole family together when decisions have to be made, and listen to what everyone has to say, even the youngest members will be proud to do their share of the work. They will accept that you have a full-time job, and even feel superior to their friends whose mums stay at home all day.

However responsible your children are, you will need to give some thought to the hours after school before you or your husband get home. There should be obligatory tasks to be carried out, even if there is no homework. Without a specific task to do boredom can set in, and that soon leads to mischief. You will have to arrange for someone to meet the younger ones from school and keep an eye on them until you get home, and also to look after them in school holidays. You will also need someone to call on for sick-room duty. You can't abandon a customer just because of measles or mumps (if it's mumps, I wouldn't even mention it at work unless you want all the men to panic!). This ideally needs to be one person rather than several different ones. Sick children want somebody familiar around, and you should keep that in mind any time you are tempted to snarl at mother-in-law!

Failing mother-in-law or a helpful neighbour, you may think of employing someone to live in. This is a big step if you have never done it before. It doesn't in fact cost that much in wages, but you have to provide decent accommodation and meals. You lose a lot of your privacy too, as no one will stay long if she is banished to her room in the evenings. You also have to share your children's affection with her, for you cannot expect her to be devoted to children who do not like her.

If you choose an au pair, you have to talk to her and allow her time to go to English classes. Au pairs will generally do some housework, but nannies do not. They look after the children and their clothes, cook for them and clean their room, but that's all. Once the children are past the baby stage, you might think of a general housekeeper instead. You can find all of these through advertisements in *The Lady*.

Don't let your children be beastly to these people, but on the other hand, do let the children know that they don't have to stay if they don't fit in. The same thing goes for day nurseries. Even pre-school children will make it plain if they are unhappy in these. Check them out carefully before you commit yourself, and be especially wary of places that have frequent changes of staff. That is usually a sign that the management is not what it might be, and it is very unsettling for young children.

All this does not sound like an easy proposition, but you have to think of such things if you make up your mind to have children and carry on working. Are you sure you want to? Have children, I mean. It isn't obligatory, you know, even if your mother and his behave as if it were. It is your body and your life, and you shouldn't let someone else talk you into breeding if you are not sure you want to.

It is hard enough running a job and your share of a home and a marriage (a term I use to include all stable relationships of a more tax-advantageous type). In fact, it is hard enough just running the job without the marriage, let alone a marriage with a difficult man. If it is your job that is making him difficult, or your success, you may have some tricky decisions on your hands. Some women feel that they should not earn more than their husband, in case it makes him feel insecure. Some husbands feel the same way, some don't. Only you can know what sort you have, and only you can decide whether you are prepared to stifle your career in order to keep your marriage together.

It may not be your earning power he resents as much as your freedom, or the opportunities he thinks you have for getting up to mischief with other men. If it really creates a problem, you have to ask yourself which you want most – the job or the husband.

It is worth taking this into account when you are looking for a mate. Once you have got used to your independence, it is awfully hard to give it up. So beware the early signs of chauvinism in your boyfriends – the ones who won't let you pay for anything, who don't want to hear about your job, who think you should drop everything to fall in with their plans. If he does this before you are married, just think what he'll be like after. What you need is a man who is emotionally secure, and preferably successful enough to have no need to regard you as a threat. Such men actually find successful women a tremendous turn-on, and they like to boast about your success to their friends. They view it as an embellishment to their own status, not as a threat.

They are about, on the loose, available for you to find if you look in the right places. Look where people play expensive games, such as polo, skiing or flying, or at meetings of the British Institute of Management, the Chamber of Commerce, conferences and trade fairs. Take your time over building a relationship and it is more likely to last than if you jump in and try to commit yourselves right away.

And do take care. Don't let your need for a mate pressurise you into dangerous or distasteful situations. Beware of married hyenas on the prowl, especially when you are travelling. You should know that there is nothing as attractive as a persuasive salesman. You probably work with a bunch of them, so keep your ear tuned for the ones who can't resist practising their selling techniques, especially on a woman! It is quite easy to stop this sort in their tracks by commenting on some aspect of their pitch as though you were criticising a role play at sales school.

It never does any harm to assert yourself in this way. Even colleagues who have no thought of getting you into bed will try to push you into female roles to boost their own egos. The problem is that it can be difficult to draw the line between assertion and aggression, especially when you realise that someone is taking liberties. The trouble with aggression is that it breeds more aggression, and that is a no-win situation when you are outnumbered by men. Any group of men, or any man who has access to a group for support, will automatically side against a woman. They will bring all the emotive anti-female expressions into play against you and you will end up looking silly.

Assertiveness is not a matter of demanding what you want with angry words and gestures. It involves feeling good about yourself, and being confident enough to ask for what you want firmly enough and persistently enough to get it. If you are not too good at getting what you want, think of going on an assertiveness-training course. These courses do a lot of work on building self-confidence, and many women who have attended them say that they had never realised before that it was OK for them to make mistakes. It is that business of not daring to take risks that paralyses so many of us.

Different organisations approach assertiveness training in a variety of ways, but they all agree that the best way to get what you want is a technique called 'broken record'. This is a calm repetition of your wishes, despite attempts to trap you by manipulative techniques or irrelevant logic. One of the classic tricks is the one used by bosses who respond to your complaints by complaining about how badly they are treated themselves. If you allow yourself to get side-tracked into making sympathetic noises, he's won, because he hasn't actually answered your complaint. What you should do is say, 'I appreciate that you have problems, but I can't do anything about them. However, you can do something about my problem, which as I told you is this.' And you keep coming back to that, no matter how many other diversions he may produce. There's nothing like sweet reason to wear down resistance.

This approach also prevents you from getting too steamed up, which is doubly counter-productive. It lets people know they can needle you – and it plays havoc with your general equilibrium. Just being a working woman is stressful enough, without adding self-inflicted wind-ups to the situation. Self-inflicted or not, you need to develop some methods of defusing your anger and reducing your stress load.

My boss has a bean bag which he flings at the wall. I've often thought lovingly of the therapeutic value of wax models and pins, but what I actually do is break pencils, reduce pieces of paper to confetti – or swear. The trouble with swearing is that you need to check first that no one shockable is within earshot, and that rather takes away the spontaneity.

The real answer to all this is to learn some good relaxation techniques and to avoid all the things that cause tension. Once you know what upsets your boss or your main customers, you would be wise to avoid doing it, thereby saving yourself some recurring hassles.

Make sure you keep your blood sugar up by eating regularly, get plenty of exercise and enough sleep. If you find that coffee keeps you awake, don't drink it in the evenings, and don't programme yourself for nightmares by reading horror stories or watching nasty films like *Jaws* or *Alien*. It is quite common for career women to dream of being chased or attacked by monsters – psychologists say this is a result of our high valuation of ourselves. It also women who are the major sufferers from phobias – another bit of genetic programming, for most phobias are related to things that would have been genuinely dangerous when we were living in the wild – animals, heights, tight spaces with no easy exit and so on. If you suffer from this tendency, it should be a comfort to you to know that it normally wears off when you reach the menopause.

Like the other skills I mentioned earlier, you will find that you can 'switch on' your relaxation mode by giving it a label. This is why meditation tutors give you a personal mantra to recite. You will find, even if you practise relaxation techniques without a tutor, that a 'trigger' phrase or word will present itself to you without your trying. Most relaxation techniques involve breathing exercises as well as visualisation. There are many breathing routines, but the most effective involves counting as you breathe in, hold your breath, breathe out and hold your breath again. The idea is to extend the counts until your whole breathing pattern is slowed. At the same time, you visualise your tension as a tangible thing that is going away from you. You could see it as a heavy cloak, that slips from your shoulders to settle round your feet; as mud, that washes away as you stand under a warm shower; or as liquid inside yourself, that drains out of your fingers and toes when you turn on the taps.

One popular technique is known as 'the quiet place' or 'your private space'. You sit or lie quietly with your eyes shut, then build yourself an imaginary place where you can go to be on your own, and where no one can interrupt you. Let's say this is at the top of a beech tree. Imagine the climb up to the top, moving from branch to branch, feeling the bark under your hands and seeing its greyish colour. When you have reached your favourite branch, settle comfortably with your back against the trunk and look around you at the twigs and leaves. Feel the cool breeze on your cheeks and let your breathing slow down to match the slow, slow pulse of the tree.

Every time you do this, make the route up the branches exactly the same, and settle in exactly the same place. You will soon find that you need do no more than think, I'll go and sit in my tree, to trigger the calmness that you achieve after the detailed climb. You may prefer floating in a mountain lake, or just sitting quietly in a nice room. It doesn't matter where it is, as long as it is the same place every time.

If disturbing thoughts intrude, deal with them in a manner appropriate to the place. In the tree, turn them into a bird and make it fly away; in the room, write them on a piece of paper and put it away in a box on a shelf behind you. This 'putting away pieces of paper' technique, or the alternative method of writing the distraction down, then snatching up the piece of paper, crumpling it and throwing it in a wastebin, is also excellent as an aid to concentration.

Concentration and relaxation are very much akin to each other. You cannot do either if your mind wanders, which is why it is a mistake to think you are relaxing when you are day-dreaming. Proper relaxation should leave you feeling recharged and full of energy to tackle your next task. Day-dreaming just makes you feel guilty.

You must have some proper relaxation time each day, and at least one proper holiday each year. The sales conference doesn't count as a holiday – there is too much shop talk and political manoeuvring going on at most of them to let anyone relax. Being constantly 'on duty' is no way to run your life. Whether you are a workaholic, or whether you burn your candle at both ends for the joy of the light it gives, all you are doing is shortening your life, which doesn't come into anyone's definition of success!

11 Moving into management

It tends to be assumed that the logical progression from super successful salesperson is to become a sales manager. If you can do it yourself, the theory goes, you can help lots of other people do it, and make more money in the process.

I have worked for many years in a senior position in the head office of a large direct sales organisation. In that time, I have seen several hundred good salespeople promoted to managers – and I have seen over three-quarters of them fail in that role. They either leave the company to try their luck as a manager somewhere else (and I subsequently hear on my grapevine that they've failed there too), or they go back to selling with their tail between their legs and a severely depleted bank balance.

I conclude, therefore, that the theory is wrong on both counts. They are linked, of course. If you can't manage your team, they won't make enough commission to make your override on it as much as you can earn on your own. Since the average override is 10 per cent, to break even means that you have to have a team of ten people, each producing as much as you did. The moral here is that you should not accept a management position unless it comes with a competent team. Management is tricky enough without the added pressure of penury caused by trying to start a team from scratch.

I am not saying that you should abandon the idea of being a manager. I am saying that you should give long and careful thought to it before you move over, and that you ought to build up a financial buffer before you do.

What it boils down to is that a manager and a salesperson are not necessarily the same animal. Often the really good salesperson is the one who is virtually addicted to the 'buzz' they get when the prospect agrees to buy. If you are one of these, unless you are sure that you will get the same buzz when one of your team brings in a big sale, you would do better to think of moving to a product that brings better commission, if more money is your goal.

Warning over. Let's get on to the positive aspect of management. Not only can you make a great deal more money by managing a good productive sales team than you can by selling yourself, if you turn out to have a talent for management *per se*, and many women do, you can move on up from managing a sales team to a senior management position at head office.

This does require a different mode of thinking, however. The immediacies of actual selling, of going out and getting today's sale, have to give way to planning on a longer-term basis and a larger geographical spread. It is 'not what you can do but what you can control'. Managing a sales team is a question of delegation – you are delegating the business of seeing customers and taking orders to others, while you concentrate on the larger tasks of selecting and training delegatees and looking for markets rather than prospects.

You will find that your pattern recognition has to change, whether you are dealing with your team or with head office. A set of responses that you recognise in a customer as meaning 'I'm going to buy' might mean 'I'm going to get away with it' in someone you are disciplining, or in a skilled political manipulator. You also have to learn to interpret the responses you get when you are interviewing recruits. A sales manager's job is often defined as 'recruit, train and motivate', with the heaviest emphasis on 'recruit'. Many organisations will provide you with subordinate managers to do the training, but they all want good recruiters.

Actual recruitment methods can vary tremendously. Some companies do it from head office, then allocate potential trainees to branches, while others give each manager an advertising budget and let them get on with it. Some insist that the recruit fills in a battery of questionnaires for head office scoring and assessment before anything else happens, while others just leave it to the managers.

However the early stages are dealt with, you are eventually going to interview the potential recruit and decide whether he will make a worthwhile member of your team. If you are working for a company that takes on inexperienced people for selling jobs, you also have to decide whether you can make a decent salesperson out of that recruit. Conducting a job interview is very different from conducting a sales interview, and this is one of the main causes of failure in the salesperson/manager transition. To sell your product you have to make your prospect so keen to have the product that they ignore the cost. With an unsuitable recruit, the cost becomes more and more apparent to them as time goes by, and their enthusiasm for the product, which in this case is the job, turns to bitterness and resentment.

If you say to a recruit, 'Our product is wonderful and it's easy to sell. Our company is wonderful and it will give you a lot of money for selling its product. If you join me I'll help you to make your fortune,' the recruit is almost certain to respond by saying, 'Wow, I'd like that. I can do the job – give it to me.' And he will then go out of his way to convince you that he can do the job, that he's just the person you want. In other words, you've sold the job to him instead of seeing if he has the ability to sell himself to you.

Your role in this interviewing situation is not to ask leading questions, but to ask open questions. Explain what the job entails, of course, but don't major on the exciting and lucrative aspects at the expense of the hard slog and rejection aspects. Then sit back and listen to what the recruit has to say.

The most successful managers in our company, by which I mean the ones whose branches have consistently been at the top of the league tables for many years and through bear and bull markets, are the ones whose recruit-interviewing technique consists of trying to put the recruit off the job. Only the most persistent and determined make it on to the initial training course, but they are the ones who stay and make a success of the job.

It is easy to decide that someone who is like you and is easy to get on with will automatically be as successful at the job as you were. It is also easy to be so keen to recruit this mirror image of yourself that you forget to probe for the real person behind your reflected image. (This is known by professional interviewers as the 'halo' effect.)

I have spent a major portion of the last year devising a recruit-selection system to solve the appalling turnover situation with recruits in our industry. On average, half of them have fallen by the wayside within one year of joining. I have looked at the records of about 5,000 people and have reached some conclusions.

The first is that you cannot devise a system to select winners – there is often a maverick streak in them that defies classification – but you can easily learn to weed out losers. The second is that leopards do not change their spots, which is how you can detect these no-hopers. And the third is that the most useful question you can ask of a potential recruit (I would suggest you don't actually ask the recruit the question, if you are fond of the shape of your nose) is, 'If you are so damn clever, why aren't you rich?'

What this boils down to is that people who are going to be successful, at whatever they set out to do, will show signs of that orientation in their previous history. The new school-leaver will have a record of sporting and academic successes, and the person who has been at work for any length of time will have a similar record of success. His changes of job will be logical and show an upward progression, his salary levels will show a steady climb, and (here's the 'why aren't you rich?' bit) he will have some material assets to show.

The person who has bounced aimlessly from job to job, from spouse to spouse, and from one piece of rented accommodation to another, is not going to settle down and work hard for you, any more than he has done for all his other bosses. The flash salesmen, and we've all seen them, with their fast cars and gold jewellery and multitudinous girlfriends, who move from selling cars to photocopiers to double glazing to car-phones, will move on again from your product as soon as the mood takes them. They may have been top salesman when they left their last job, but they often move on before the complaints start to come in, and you do not want to join the ranks of their ex-managers who spend half their time placating Sonnyboy's unhappy victims. It is going to take all of your non-recruiting time to keep your team happy and motivated and bringing in the bacon, without wasting any of it dodging the flak that comes from poor selection, so do yourself a favour and don't recruit trouble.

The simplistic view of motivation is that there is nothing like the stick and the carrot. They earn their own carrots, but you apply the stick; or to put it another way, nothing works as hard as a hungry salesman. With some people this is true. I know managers who deliberately encourage their team members to take on more and more financial commitments – car-phone, computers, membership of this and that club, children in private schools, a bigger and better car or house – merely because all those commitments keep the man (it's usually a man who falls for this routine) working hard to pay for them.

For every man who responds that way, however, there are others (and a lot of women) who become so paralysed with worry about all the money they owe that they cannot work at all; and others who don't care about the money as much as being top of the league table every year; and others who don't give a damn about any of that stuff as long as they get their daily fix of customers saying, 'Yes, I'll buy.'

So we come back to your role as dream merchant – only this time the dream is not what the product will do for the customer, but what selling the product will do for the salesperson. Your role as sales manager is to identify and encourage whichever version of that dream will best motivate each member of your team – and then to give whatever practical help you can towards making the dream come true.

Don't forget that most people, and especially men, want not only to be successful in their own right, but to be a member of the winning team. The person who is an exceptional success in a team of mediocre performers is always vulnerable to approaches from competitors who will say, 'What's a star like you doing with that load of bums?' You'll have trouble keeping him, and you'll also have mutterings from your rival managers who will say, 'Oh sure, she's top of the league this year, but that's only because she's lucky enough to have the brilliant Bloggs on her team!'

So it's up to you to persuade your people that they are a team, not a collection of individuals, and then to persuade them that they can – and *will* – (think positive) be the winning team. If you can create the vision of success as something attainable, they will all work towards it. Your main problem will be in achieving the right balance between the praise your star performers think is their right, and the praise that is needed to encourage beginners. I have been at monthly meetings where the manager has been giving out prizes for production, and as the names are called out down the line, you can feel the resentment and depression from the people in the back row.

'Number twenty – it's Henry Higgins. Never mind Henry, better luck next month,' says the manager, and poor Henry blushes and averts his gaze. Surely the manager could have found something encouraging to say to Henry? How about, 'A special round of applause for Henry Higgins. He hasn't been with us very long, but this month he sold his first multi-widget grinder. Well done, Henry – keep them coming!'

This technique is known as 'catch them doing something right', and it is a better carrot than money. Everyone likes to be praised, but how often do we get it? You get told quickly enough when you do things wrong, but how are you meant to know you've got it right unless someone tells you? So tell your team you are pleased with them, and they'll get that warm glow of pleasure three times. Once when you tell them, a second time when they get home and tell their family, and a third time when they get up the next morning and think, 'My boss was pleased with me yesterday – I'll try and do the same thing today and she'll be pleased with me again!'

This doesn't mean that you have to spend all your time bouncing around wagging your tail to let people know you are pleased with them. Sometimes you are going to have to apply criticism and discipline, or even to fire someone. These unpleasant tasks can't be shirked, or they will all conclude that you are weak and try to take advantage of you. It may even be a good idea to wield the big stick soon after you take on the job, to let them all know you're tough enough to do it.

Just be careful how you do it. 'Tough dame' is a useful image. 'Ball-breaking bitch' isn't. The trick is to be specific rather than general with your criticism. So instead of saying, 'Your performance is slipping,' which implies that the person is failing, you say, 'You haven't sold anything this week,' which means that they did OK before and will probably do OK again, but this week was not good and you don't like it.

There is no need to get involved in their excuses for a bad performance. You don't want excuses, you want the performance you know they are capable of, and you need to let them know that. Do your broken-record assertive act: 'You know you're good and I know you're good, but this week wasn't up to scratch.' Then you send them away feeling good: 'I'm sure you'll be back on form next week. I'm hoping you'll be with us at the convention this year.'

Let that be the end of it, unless the poor performance becomes such a habit that you feel you have to fire the person concerned. There is little point in wasting your time on a no-hoper, and you really do have to get rid of them in the interests of good housekeeping. Not only will you be thought weak if you don't do it, but people who don't pull their weight irritate the whole team. And there is nothing as demotivating as having a loser around all the time. Losers tend to winge on about how it's not their fault, then they winge on about whose fault it is (you, the company, the training department, the product, the customers . . .), and pretty soon the rest of the team will begin to complain about these things as well.

Firing people is not nice, but it has to be done. Managers who have to do it a lot say the trick is to find something personal you dislike about the person (their clothes, their religion, an irritating habit), and focus on that as a reason why they deserve to be fired. General incompetence is probably the real reason, but it isn't quite as easy to get worked up about as smelly armpits. You don't let them know about this, of course, nor do you surprise them by blurting out that they're fired without any preamble. Most people know it's coming anyway, and actually find it a relief when you finally tell them you have concluded that they would be better suited working in another environment.

In a self-employed direct sales situation, what happens more often is that they just fade away. They stop coming into the office every day, then they stop coming to the monthly meetings and fail to respond to your telephone messages or letters. Then all you need do is tell head office to send the official termination letter and take their names off the league board.

The situations where you have a really nasty confrontation at a firing interview are fortunately very rare. If you expect one of these it is a good idea to have a witness, for acrimonious confrontations have a nasty habit of turning into court cases or industrial tribunals, and you don't want there to be any arguments over who said what. In fact, the less you say the better. Remember – a closed mouth gathers no foot.

Apart from these 'exit' interviews, the most likely cause for acrimony in the office will be the prima donnas on your team. If they are really consistently brilliant performers, you may be inclined to tolerate their demanding behaviour, especially if discipline will affect that performance. On the other hand, you may believe that no one is entitled to behave badly, no matter who they are. Take the precaution of checking with your boss first, though, or you may find El Brillianto has gone over your head to get what he wants. He may also incite the rest of the team to gang up on you, so be careful.

Oddly enough, although they will always threaten to do so, these prima donnas will rarely actually leave the company to go to a competitor. They realise that it isn't that easy to explain to a large client bank, for example, why you have changed your mind about which is the best product on the market. And there is always the doubt in their mind that the competitor might already have someone as good or, horrors, maybe even better! So it might just be worth calling his bluff. Even if he does go, you'll have his client list to distribute to the rest of the team, and they will be delighted to have him out of the way. He may try to take some of them with him, but the ones that go in this sort of situation are rarely much of a loss.

But why let a good producer go if all you need to do is learn to handle him? It isn't necessary that you should like him, or even that he should like you, as long as you can tolerate each other. That applies to the whole team. You are there to get a job done, not win a popularity contest. The job is to keep the sales rolling in, at an ever-increasing level. They must increase by at least the level of inflation, or you will be going downhill in real terms. I have known high-earning sales managers with stable teams of steady producers get fired because they were on a plateau when the management wanted to see big percentage increases. So it's up to you to keep your team climbing, by whatever means it takes.

It may not have occurred to you, if you have never studied management, that there are various types of leadership styles. These fall into two basic categories – autocratic or democratic – which are known in management training circles as Theory X and Theory Y. Theory X assumes that people will only work if they are made to. Theory Y assumes that people work because they actually like to.

If you are a Theory X manager, you will want to take charge and tell your team what to do all the time. You may fit in well running a team of representatives selling FMCGs to retailers, but you will not last long with a team of high-earning direct sales people. They are Theory Y people and will not tolerate anyone other than a Theory Y manager. They will expect to be consulted before major decisions affecting them are made, and they will respond better to 'Let's work together' than 'Do as you're told!'. They will also see very quickly if you are not as good at your job of managing as they are at theirs of selling, and you will lose their respect. It won't matter that you were brilliant at selling yourself. You don't do that now, you manage, and all they will see is that you're not very good at it.

You will help yourself tremendously by keeping a measure of distance between yourself and them. Don't try to be 'one of the lads', but stay a little aloof. Keep your domestic problems to yourself, and don't let your enquiries into their well-being and the success of their weekend degenerate into gossip.

Watch your body language. Remember that powerful people keep still and that they stand (or sit) up straight and look people in the eye. They initiate touching and they consider themselves entitled to take over another's space. They give the impression of being bigger. If this means you have to wear high heels (not teetery ones) and padded shoulders, do so. If it means rearranging your office to allow you to dominate visitors, do it.

Do make people come into your office to see you; then they will be on your territory, which is always a situation of advantage. Remember that the more important you are, the less work will be visible, so clear your desk before they come in. You can actually be quite abrupt when you ask them to come in – that always makes people search their conscience – as long as you are nice to them when they arrive.

This is the point of all these dominance ploys. Get them right, and you will have the edge on people without having to be nasty. You will be seen as a Theory Y manager, but you will achieve your goal of producing the results from your sales team.

Postscript

So there it is. Success in selling, or in sales management, is there waiting for you to go out and get it. There is nothing in your gender to bar you, and much in it to help you. But you have got to go and get it yourself. No one will give it to you because you are a good girl who deserves it. There are no short cuts, no magic tricks that bring in the orders – just a series of techniques that have to be mastered and practised until they become second nature, then all it takes is hard work and some positive thinking.

Eliminate the loser words like 'difficult' and 'impossible' from your vocabulary, and train yourself instead to work out ways to achieve your goals. Visualise them achieved, in your imagination, and you will 'set' your mind into the winning mode. If you have to play-act a little along the way, that's fine, as long as you don't fall into the trap of believing that your own hype is true. Play-acting is one thing, total miscasting is another and will lead you into corners you can't get out of.

You may have to take some risks, but that is the only way you'll get the big rewards. To make omelettes, you have to break eggs – but you can have a lot of fun in the process!

Appendix

Women's networks: for a complete list write for the booklet entitled 'Women's Organisations in Great Britain' to the Women's National Commission, Government Offices, Great George Street, London SW1. Two of the best that have come to my attention are: Network, 25 Park Road, London NW1 6XN and Women in Management, 74 Cottenham Park Road, London SW20 0TB.

Phoenix Programme: details from the Faculty of Management, Polytechnic of Central London, 35 Marylebone Road, London NW1 5LS.

Select bibliography

These are some of the books which have helped formulate my thinking, and some others which you may find useful.

Ardrey, R., *African Genesis* (Collins, 1963)
——, *The Territorial Imperative* (Collins, 1967)
——, *Hunting Hypothesis* (Collins, 1976)
Barash, D., *Sociobiology – the Whisperings Within* (Fontana, 1981)
Berne, E., *Games People Play* (Grove Press, 1964)
——, *What Do You Say After You Say Hello?* (Corgi, 1975)
Blakeslee, T. R., *The Right Brain* (Macmillan Press, 1980)
Blanchard, K. and Johnson, S., *The One-Minute Manager* (Fontana, 1983)
Bollies, R. N., *What Colour is your Parachute?* (Ten Speed Press, 1983)
Buzan, T., *Use Your Head* (BBC Publications, 1974)
——, *Use Both Sides of your Brain* (E.P. Dutton, 1976)
——, *Speed Reading* (David and Charles, 1977)
——, *Speed Memory* (David and Charles, 1977)
Conran, S., *Superwoman* (Sidgwick and Jackson, 1975)
Durden-Smith, J. and de Simone, D., *Sex and the Brain* (Pan, 1983)
Fenton, J., *How to Sell Against Competition* (Heinemann, 1984)
Fensterheim and Dell, *Don't Say Yes When You Want*

To Say No (Dell Books, 1975)

Harris, T. A., *I'm OK/You're OK* (Pan, 1970)

Heller, R., *The Naked Market* (Sidgwick and Jackson, 1984)

Kennedy, G., *Everything is Negotiable* (Business Books, Hutchinson, 1982)

Korda, M., *Power in the Office* (Weidenfeld and Nicholson, 1975)

Lakein, A., *How to Get Control of Your Time and Your Life* (Peter H. Wyden, 1973)

Lidstone, J. (ed.), *Profitable Selling* (Wildwood House, 1986)

McCormack, Mark H., *What They Don't Teach You At Harvard Business School* (Collins, 1984)

Morris, D., *The Human Zoo* (Jonathan Cape, 1969)

——, *The Naked Ape* (Mayflower, 1977)

——, *Manwatching* (Panther, 1978)

Pease, Allan, *Body Language* (Sheldon Press, 1981)

Russell, P., *The Brain Book* (Routledge and Kegan Paul, 1979)

Sweeney, Neil R., *Managing a Sales Team* (Kogan Page, 1982)

Trisler, Hank, *No Bull Selling* (Bantam, 1983)

Video Arts, *So You Think You Can Sell?* (Methuen, 1985)

Index

A Selected List of Non-Fiction Available from Mandarin Books

While every effort is made to keep prices low, it is sometimes necessary to increase prices at short notice. Mandarin Paperbacks reserves the right to show new retail prices on covers which may differ from those previously advertised in the text or elsewhere.

The prices shown below were correct at the time of going to press.

☐	7493 0000 0	**Moonwalk**	Michael Jackson	£3.99
☐	7493 0004 3	**South Africa**	Graham Leach	£3.99
☐	7493 0010 8	**What Fresh Hell is This?**	Marion Meade	£3.99
☐	7493 0011 6	**War Games**	Thomas Allen	£3.99
☐	7493 0013 2	**The Crash**	Mihir Bose	£4.99
☐	7493 0014 0	**The Demon Drink**	Jancis Robinson	£4.99
☐	7493 0015 9	**The Health Scandal**	Vernon Coleman	£4.99
☐	7493 0016 7	**Vietnam – The 10,000 Day War**	Michael Maclear	£3.99
☐	7493 0049 3	**The Spycatcher Trial**	Malcolm Turnbull	£3.99
☐	7493 0022 1	**The Super Saleswoman**	Janet Macdonald	£4.99
☐	7493 0023 X	**What's Wrong With Your Rights?**	Cook/Tate	£4.99
☐	7493 0024 8	**Mary and Richard**	Michael Burn	£3.50
☐	7493 0061 2	**Voyager**	Yeager/Rutan	£3.99
☐	7493 0060 4	**The Fashion Conspiracy**	Nicholas Coleridge	£3.99
☐	7493 0027 2	**Journey Without End**	David Bolton	£3.99
☐	7493 0028 0	**The Common Thread**	Common Thread	£4.99

All these books are available at your bookshop or newsagent, or can be ordered direct from the publisher. Just tick the titles you want and fill in the form below.

Mandarin Paperbacks, Cash Sales Department, PO Box 11, Falmouth, Cornwall TR10 9EN.

Please send cheque or postal order, no currency, for purchase price quoted and allow the following for postage and packing:

UK   55p for the first book, 22p for the second book and 14p for each additional book ordered to a maximum charge of £1.75.

BFPO and Eire   55p for the first book, 22p for the second book and 14p for each of the next seven books, thereafter 8p per book.

Overseas   £1.00 for the first book plus 25p per copy for each additional book.
Customers

NAME (Block Letters) ....

ADDRESS ....

....